Federal Aid to Detroit

Thomas J. Anton

Federal Aid to Detroit

THE BROOKINGS INSTITUTION
Washington, D.C.

Library of Congress Catalog Card Number 82-74099
ISBN 0-8157-0437-2

This is a slightly condensed version of a report published by the U.S. Department of Labor. The report, which contains some tables not included here, is available in paper or microfiche from the National Technical Information Service, U.S. Department of Commerce, Springfield, Virginia 22161. To order, specify *Case Studies of the Impact of Federal Aid on Major Cities: City of Detroit*, order number PB-81-240-095.

THE BROOKINGS INSTITUTION is an independent organization devoted to nonpartisan research, education, and publication in economics, government, foreign policy, and the social sciences generally. Its principal purposes are to aid in the development of sound public policies and to promote public understanding of issues of national importance.

The Institution was founded on December 8, 1927, to merge the activities of the Institute for Government Research, founded in 1916, the Institute of Economics, founded in 1922, and the Robert Brookings Graduate School of Economics and Government, founded in 1924.

The Board of Trustees is responsible for the general administration of the Institution, while the immediate direction of the policies, program, and staff is vested in the President, assisted by an advisory committee of the officers and staff. The by-laws of the Institution state: "It is the function of the Trustees to make possible the conduct of scientific research, and publication, under the most favorable conditions, and to safeguard the independence of the research staff in the pursuit of their studies and in the publication of the results of such studies. It is not a part of their function to determine, control, or influence the conduct of particular investigations or the conclusions reached."

The President bears final responsibility for the decision to publish a manuscript as a Brookings book. In reaching his judgment on the competence, accuracy, and objectivity of each study, the President is advised by the director of the appropriate research program and weighs the views of a panel of expert outside readers who report to him in confidence on the quality of the work. Publication of a work signifies that it is deemed a competent treatment worthy of public consideration but does not imply endorsement of conclusions or recommendations.

The Institution maintains its position of neutrality on issues of public policy in order to safeguard the intellectual freedom of the staff. Hence interpretations or conclusions in Brookings publications should be understood to be solely those of the authors and should not be attributed to the Institution, to its trustees, officers, or other staff members, or to the organizations that support its research.

Foreword

In the 1960s and 1970s, American cities became heavy users of grants-in-aid from the federal government. The amount of that aid increased under presidents of both parties, though with differences of approach among different administrations. The Democratic administrations of Lyndon B. Johnson and Jimmy Carter sought to concentrate federal aid on large cities with the highest levels of social and economic distress, while Republican presidents Richard M. Nixon and Gerald R. Ford, seeking to devolve power to local and state governments, advocated broad-gauged formula grants to a wide range of eligible governments. Today, almost all local governments in the country use federal grants-in-aid, but the biggest cities remain the primary users, judging by the relative size of their grants and by the share of their budgets supported by federal grants.

To assess how the increasing flow of federal grants was affecting local government and politics, the Governmental Studies Program of the Brookings Institution in 1978 undertook a series of case studies in large cities with financial support from the U.S. Department of Labor and Department of Commerce. Richard P. Nathan, then a senior fellow in the Governmental Studies Program, and James W. Fossett, then a research assistant in Governmental Studies, directed the project. Under their supervision, knowledgeable local observers—many of whom had been field associates in previous Brookings research on how federal programs worked on the local level—prepared individual reports. Ten reports were distributed, beginning in 1979, by the National Technical Information Service of the Commerce Department.

The Brookings Institution is pleased to publish Mr. Fossett's summary and interpretation of the case studies, *Federal Aid to Big*

Cities: The Politics of Dependence, and slightly condensed and updated versions of selected cases, including this study of Detroit.

The central question that the project as a whole explores is to what extent large cities have become dependent on the federal government as a source of revenue. Synthesizing the findings from Detroit and other cities, Mr. Fossett's summary argues that the answer depends on how a city uses aid, which in turn depends more than anything else on the city's fiscal condition, the amount of discretion it has in using federal funds, and the level of political organization among the beneficiaries of federal programs.

Mr. Nathan, a ten-year veteran of Brookings' resident staff, is currently director of the Princeton Urban and Regional Research Center at the Woodrow Wilson School for Public and International Affairs, Princeton University, and a member of Brookings' associated staff. Mr. Fossett is a staff member at the Institute of Government and Public Affairs and the Department of Political Science at the University of Illinois.

The findings of Mr. Fossett and the case study authors are theirs alone and should not be ascribed to the Department of Labor or the Department of Commerce, or to the trustees, officers, or staff members of the Brookings Institution.

Bruce K. MacLaury
President

Washington, D.C.
March 1983

Contents

Preface   xi

1. The Setting   1

2. Federal Aid, Fiscal 1978   17

3. Employment Effects   32

4. Program Benefits   40

5. Political Effects   44

6. Conclusions   50

7. Epilog   52

Tables

1. Federal, State, and Total Revenues,
   Fiscal Years 1975–78   19

2. Federal Funds to Detroit and Overlying
   Governments, Fiscal Year 1978   22

3. Estimated Expenditures from Federal Sources,
   Detroit and Related Governments, Fiscal 1978   25

4. Detroit's Revenues from State, Fiscal Years 1975–78   26

5. Appropriations for Programs in Equity Package,
   Fiscal 1977–80   28

6. Federally Supported and Total Positions,
   Five Common Services, 1978   29

7. Summary of Positions Budgeted, Fiscal 1978,
   by Funding Source   34

8. Detroit Income Distribution   41

9. Percentage Distribution of Federal Program Benefits
   by Income Group, Fiscal 1978   42

Preface

The major reductions in grant programs to state and local governments brought about by the Reagan administration have reopened a long-standing debate about the extent to which state and local governments in general, and big cities in particular, have become "dependent" on the federal government as a source of revenue. A number of observers, noting the substantial build-up of direct federal grants to cities relative to other revenue sources during the 1970s, have argued that cities have increasingly come to rely on federal funds as a source of support for ongoing city activities. The July 1982 urban policy report by the Reagan administration argued that the continuing availability of large amounts of federal funds has made local officials more politically responsive to Washington than to their constituents, has distorted local budget and program priorities, and has interfered with the operation of market forces.[1]

The changes in federal grants to cities over the 1970s were indeed substantial. The most important change was a major increase in the amount of such aid. In 1970, the federal government made $1.3 billion in direct grants to cities; by 1978, this figure was more than six times as large. Because the amount of revenue that cities were raising from local taxes only doubled during that period, the federal government became the source of an increased share of the total budget for many cities. The Advisory Commission on Intergovernmental Relations estimates that in 1967 federal grants to forty-seven of the nation's largest cities were

---

1. U.S. Department of Housing and Urban Development, *The President's National Urban Policy Report, 1982* (Washington, D.C.: U.S. Government Printing Office, 1982).

equal to 10 percent of the funds that those cities taken together raised from their own sources; by 1978, that figure was 50 percent.

Changes occurred over the same period in the geographic distribution of federal funds. Under many of the Great Society programs of the 1960s, cities had to apply to different federal agencies for funds under each category of aid; the agencies allocated the money to the cities that submitted what were judged to be the strongest applications. This method tended to concentrate grants in larger cities, especially in the Northeast, which invested effort in preparing proposals and lobbying for their approval. Under the Nixon administration's New Federalism—the centerpiece of which was general revenue sharing, enacted in 1972—and the Carter administration's $13.5 billion economic stimulus package, enacted in 1977, by contrast, funds were parceled out under formula distribution systems to cities that met the eligibility criteria of the formula. This approach tended to spread funds out to cities that in the past had received little or no federal money. Among the large cities, the major beneficiaries of this change were in the South and West.

The increase in federal funding for cities was accompanied by a shift in the locus of control over these funds within cities. The programs of the 1950s and 1960s channeled substantial amounts of money into organizations that in many cases were outside the regular city government, such as community action agencies and urban renewal authorities. The programs of the seventies, by contrast, gave substantial discretion to elected officials of general-purpose city governments. Local agencies that in the past submitted their own applications to Washington had to start working through city hall to obtain federal aid. Leaders of community groups with special interests in certain programs now have to deal with city councils and mayors to ensure that their interests are served.

A number of analysts have contended that these changes led many cities to become both economically and politically "dependent" on federal funds, both as a source of financial support for city activities and as a source of political capital for local elected officials. Some of these analysts examine the ratio of federal aid dollars to locally raised dollars—in some large cities as much as one federal dollar for every two locally raised dollars. Other analysts concerned with "dependence" perform econometric studies whose results suggest that cities use federal funds for activities that would have been supported with local money if the federal aid had not been available. Some observers also suggest that the local constituencies that have built up for several federally aided activities would make it politically difficult, if not impossible, for local officials to discontinue these activities if federal funds were to be withdrawn.

From this body of findings, many observers have drawn gloomy conclusions about the consequences of major cuts in federal aid. Most cities lack enough locally raised current revenues to continue more than a small fraction of the services supported by federal aid, and would be forced either to raise taxes substantially or to cut services drastically if that aid were reduced. Some analysts have further argued that such reductions would force local governments to draw down surpluses accumulated as a result of previous increases in federal support, thus harming cities' financial positions and credit ratings.

There are two reasons for suspecting that this scenario is too pessimistic. First, it is far from clear that the total amount of federal money a city receives relative to its own revenues is a reasonable measure of the importance of federal funds, or that a city receiving a large amount of federal money relative to its own revenues is more "dependent" on those funds than another city with relatively less federal aid. Both the amount of federal aid a particular city receives and the amount it raises on its own are affected by the range of functions for which the city government is responsible, the level of services it provides, the cost of providing these services, and the amount of support it receives from the state and from other governments, such as an overlying county. Differences among cities in the ratio of federal to local revenues may reflect differences in these other factors rather than differences in the degree of "dependence" on federal aid.

Second—and more important—many cities have been more cautious about how they use federal dollars than the conventional view suggests. Rather than merging federal money into the general revenue stream, local officials often try to reduce the risks involved from potential aid cutbacks by separating federal dollars from other revenues. They use federal money for capital projects, nonrecurring operating activities, and other activities that could be readily discontinued if aid were terminated. Some cities with pressing financial difficulties have used federal funds to support ongoing city services, but there is no reason to assume that all cities have done so.

In brief, how a city uses federal aid—not the overall size of that aid—is the most appropriate measure of the city's "dependence" on federal money. A city that uses large amounts of federal funds for such basic services as police protection, garbage collection, and street repairs is more likely to have trouble adjusting to aid cutbacks than is a city that has segregated federal dollars from the rest of the local budget and used them for activities that officials consider less central. Because voters expect a city to provide adequate levels of basic services, a city that relies heavily on federal aid to provide those services must either raise taxes or reduce service levels if that aid were cut back. The same is not always true of other types of activities.

Clearly, an informed judgment on the extent to which cities are "dependent" on federal aid requires attention to the uses to which cities have put that aid and the availability of local resources to continue the activities supported by such aid. The research supporting the conventional view of "dependence" does not provide such an assessment. In all the calculations of the ratio of federal to local dollars and in the statistical estimates of the impact of grant funds on aggregate levels of local taxes and expenditures, little attempt has been made to identify the types of programs cities have funded with federal money or to define how cities with different patterns of spending vary in their political or financial characteristics.

This case study of the impact of federal grants on the city of Detroit is one in a series of studies, undertaken by the Governmental Studies Program at The Brookings Institution, that are intended to provide evidence on these questions. This study was prepared by Thomas J. Anton, professor of political science at the University of Michigan. The period of observation was fiscal year 1978, when federal grants to cities were at their peak.

The authors of the case studies used a common framework, focusing on three main issues. The first was the extent to which each city had become dependent on federal grants to pay for basic city services. Each case study not only reports the share of the city budget supported by federal dollars, but also assesses city policies for using federal dollars; the types of services supported by federal grants; the ease with which cities could replace federal funds; and how strongly constituents supported the activities financed with federal dollars. Particular attention was devoted to each city's use of funds provided under the Carter administration's economic stimulus package, which was the major source of new federal funds provided to cities during fiscal 1978.

The second major issue that these studies address is the politics surrounding the allocation of federal grants within each city. As noted earlier, aid programs of the 1970s gave local elected officials more authority over how to spend federal dollars than had been given by previous programs. Under some circumstances, however, elected officials may not want to become actively involved in deciding what to do with federal funds, for fear that possible cutbacks in federal funds would force them to make unpopular decisions. These case studies describe the political process by which federal money is allocated in each city, identify the persons and groups who play roles in this process, and assess how the growth in federal aid during the 1970s affected local decision making and politics.

The final issue these studies consider is the distribution of benefits from federally supported programs. Federal programs vary widely in the extent to which they require local governments to focus federally funded activities on particular income groups or areas within the city. These studies report on how the benefits have been spread.

By reporting on how cities responded to the major build-up in federal grants during the 1970s, these studies provide a useful baseline by which to assess the effects of the reductions in grant programs made by the Reagan administration. A major study is under way at the Princeton Urban and Regional Research Center, Princeton University, to identify these effects on the governments and residents of fourteen states, fourteen large cities, and twenty-six suburban and rural jurisdictions.[2] Nine of the cities examined in the case study research undertaken by Brookings are included in the Princeton study: Boston, Chicago, Cleveland, Houston, Los Angeles, Phoenix, Rochester, St. Louis, and Tulsa.

In this case study, Anton portrays Detroit as a city in deep economic trouble. It is dominated by the automobile industry; most jobs are in companies that make cars and trucks or their components. Because the city's residential areas grew up around large factories that were scattered throughout the city, Detroit lacks a strong downtown of the sort that many other cities have—one that attracts large numbers of firms that need to be near each other for convenient face-to-face contacts.

2. Initial findings of the Princeton study have been published in John W. Ellwood, ed., *Reductions in U.S. Domestic Spending: How They Affect State and Local Governments* (New Brunswick, N.J.: Transaction Books, 1982).

Although many of Detroit's residents earn high wages won by strong industrial unions, an exodus of whites from the city to the suburbs in the 1960s and 1970s left the city with much higher proportions of low-income and black families than its surrounding areas. The city's historic reliance on a single industry has prevented it from overcoming this disadvantage. The city suffers more from recessions than does the nation as a whole, and many workers who have only the skills needed in industrial plants—or who have no skills at all—cannot fill the jobs available in the service sector. Over the past two decades, the city has seen the growth of an "underclass" of structurally unemployed people. At the same time, its buildings and public facilities have been deteriorating, and its tax base has been shrinking.

Efforts to deal with Detroit's problems through governmental action have depended on the political situation at each level of government. Most success has been achieved at the local level, where Mayor Coleman A. Young has been able to win the trust and support of the city's business elite while keeping the backing of his more natural constituencies, blacks and liberal labor unions. Racial animosity and the desire of suburban leaders to benefit from the city's loss of jobs and populations have hindered attempts at regional cooperation. At the state level, the personal support of Gov. William G. Milliken helped bring about expansion of state aid for the city during the 1970s despite opposition from the governor's fellow Republicans in the state legislature.

The most notable efforts to apply governmental resources to the city's needs have been Mayor Young's successes in attracting federal aid in various forms. The mayor was not solely responsible for the jump of 62 percent in federal aid to the city between fiscal 1975 and fiscal 1978—much of this aid was from revenue sharing and other block grant programs that allocated money by formulas—but his city government was well organized and quick to make the city's needs heard in Washington.

Anton identifies the following major effects of federal aid:

1. Detroit received nearly $400 million in federal aid in fiscal 1978, spending almost $269 million of it that year. More than 70 percent of the federal dollars spent by the city were for operating purposes.

2. Overlying governments and special districts serving Detroit received another $77 million.

3. The city has become highly dependent on federal aid. The $269 million in federal money that the city spent in 1978 was

almost as much as it raised from all local taxes and assessments—$282 million. All types of city services—even the most basic ones, such as police, fire, and sanitation—used federal aid as part of their general revenues, lumping federal funds in with locally raised revenue.

4. An estimated 27 percent of all city employees were paid with funds that can be directly traced to federal aid programs. Almost all the city's departments used some workers funded by federal aid, including the public service employment (PSE) program.

5. The public service employment program was the portion of the Carter economic stimulus package that provided help at the most critical time—the depth of the 1974-75 recession. This aid "helped keep the city alive during that trying period," when unemployment hit 17.4 percent. The peak of unemployment had passed by the time antirecession fiscal assistance became available, but this aid did allow the city to keep reductions in the number of full-time city employees to 2,000 between 1975 and 1976. Grants for local public works contributed to several construction projects that were crucial to the city's efforts to bring about a downtown "renaissance."

6. Low- and moderate-income families made up about one-third of the city's population, but were the main beneficiaries of about two-thirds of the federally aided programs. In the case of the PSE program, the direct beneficiaries—those who held PSE jobs—were primarily those with relatively high incomes, because many of these positions were used to rehire laid-off city workers at their old salaries.

7. During the late 1970s, when amounts of federal aid were increasing, Mayor Young was able to mesh local public works and urban development action grant efforts to build a coalition of labor and business interests around downtown renovation projects. At the same time, he used community development block grant funds to support improvements in the neighborhoods. The result overall has been to strengthen the mayor's political position enormously and to centralize decisions on the city's development strategy. The mayor's success in these efforts was due in equal parts to his own dynamism and to the availability of federal funds; if the flow of money dries up, even the most dynamic mayor may find further development difficult.

We are pleased to acknowledge contributions to the case study project by several persons. We would like particularly to acknowledge research assistance by Claire C. Osborn and a great deal of useful advice on municipal finances from Philip M. Dearborn, vice president of the Greater Washington Research Center. We would also like to acknowledge the contributions of the local officials and academics who reviewed earlier drafts and provided many useful comments for the revision process. Dr. Anton was assisted in his research by Richard Schwartz.

David L. Aiken of the Princeton Urban and Regional Research Center prepared the manuscript for publication, with the assistance of Mary Capouya. Hannah Kaufman of the Princeton University Computer Center helped with computer-based production. Finally, we would like to express our appreciation to Seymour Brandwein, director of the Office of Program Evaluation of the Employment and Training Administration, U.S. Department of Labor, for his advice, assistance, and encouragement on this project.

October 1982

Richard P. Nathan
Princeton, New Jersey
James W. Fossett
Urbana, Illinois

1. The Setting

The city of Detroit enters the 1980s as the nation's leading experiment in urban political change. This status does not arise from historical experiences that are radically different from those of other older, industrialized American cities. As we shall see, demographic trends in and around Detroit during the past several decades are quite similar to changes in other metropolitan areas. What makes Detroit different is a remarkable fusion of the city's elite into a coherent leadership structure, complete with goals, strategies, and tactics. Politically, Detroit has its act together. The question that will be answered in the next several years is whether intelligent and well-organized local leadership will make any real difference to the city's future development. At the moment, that is an open question.

How the question is answered will depend to a very considerable extent on future trends in federal aid to Detroit. During the 1970s federal assistance grew rapidly, reaching nearly $270 million in 1978, when federal funds were by far the largest single source of revenue available to the city. Federal assistance to Detroit is no longer expanding, but the federal presence remains large, and the city thus remains highly dependent on federal funds. Whether or not Detroit's fiscal dependence on federal funds has implied programmatic or political dependence is less clear. Who controls the actual use of dollars is a function not only of their source, but also of the forms in which the dollars are given, the organizational setting in which the dollars are received, and the skills of both givers and receivers. This study explores these relationships with a view toward understanding the effects of federal aid on local governmental capacity in Detroit. Understanding those effects is essential if we are to appreciate the past impact and future potential of federal assistance to this old but still vibrant city.

The City's Development

Although founded in 1701 and incorporated in 1806, Detroit did not develop into a major metropolitan center until the twentieth century, when the manufacture of automobiles became a major component of the American economy. Unlike major East Coast cities, Detroit never developed according to a European city model, in which a clearly delineated downtown provided a focus for a major commercial, cultural, and residential location. Instead Detroit developed as a "spread city," with residential neighborhoods made up mostly of single-family houses springing up around industrial plants located some distance from the city center. As population expanded, new neighborhoods were created in areas even more distant from the city center, and along with them the infrastructure of streets, water and sewer lines, and neighborhood commercial strips to service neighborhood populations. "Downtown" contained city and county government offices, the law firms associated with such activity, and a few banks, but corporate headquarters for the city's principal industry were all some miles away: Ford in suburban Dearborn, Chrysler in Highland Park, General Motors in the "new center" area several miles north on Woodward Avenue.[1] Since few other major industries existed in Detroit, there was little opportunity for the downtown area to provide a setting for the variegated face-to-face contacts that Raymond Vernon, among others, has identified as an important stimulus to downtown development.[2] As Detroit grew, neighborhoods—some of them quite distinct—were spread across 140 square miles but downtown remained somewhat nondescript, reminiscent of Gertrude Stein's comment about another place: "There was no 'there' there."

It is at least conceivable that the absence of a well-defined sense of place in Detroit has contributed to the striking volatility of the city's population during the past eighty years. In a perceptive reminiscence of his own years in Detroit, William Serrin recently

---

1. See Robert E. Conot, *American Odyssey* (New York: Morrow Publishers, 1974) for an interesting review of Detroit's history.

2. Raymond Vernon, *The Changing Economic Function of the Central City* (New York: Area Development Committee, Council on Economic Development, 1959). See also Jane Jacobs, *The Economy of Cities* (New York: Vintage, 1970).

suggested that Detroit has always been a place that people went in order to earn money—but left as soon as they could, either to return home (often the South) or to move to someplace better outside the city itself.[3] During the formative second and third decades of this century more than a million new residents came to Detroit, and another quarter-million were added in the 1940s, as war production stimulated employment growth. Since 1950, however, large numbers of people have been fleeing Detroit. Between 1970 and 1980, the census count dropped by one-fifth, from 1.5 million to 1.2 million.

Why have so many people abandoned the city, and why do others continue to do so in such impressive numbers? Serrin's insight suggests part of the answer. Earlier population expansion was due almost entirely to the rapid development of heavy industry, particularly the manufacture of automobiles and related parts or supplies such as tires. Pursuit of employment in these industries or in the smaller but significant tool and die, fixture, foundry, or pharmaceutical industries, led hundreds of thousands of workers to the city. Many of these jobs continue to exist in Detroit, but expansion of industrial or commercial employment since 1950 has taken place almost entirely in the suburbs around Detroit. In 1948, most of the metropolitan area's manufacturing, wholesale, and retail employment was located in the city; by 1977, most of these jobs were located outside Detroit itself. Federal government decisions to build a vast highway network through and around the city made decentralization possible; decisions by corporations such as General Motors to locate large new facilities in the suburbs provided employment incentives; decisions by other corporations such as B.L. Smokler Co. and Chrysler Realty provided suburban housing opportunities (subsidized by federal tax incentives); and the choice made by the area's largest retailer, the J.L. Hudson Co., to "ring" the city with a series of huge shopping centers provided the commercial service facilities necessary to support the needs of new suburban residents. To a considerable extent, then, people have left Detroit because jobs, houses, and shopping opportunities increasingly have been located in the suburban fringe. By 1976 fewer than a third of metropolitan area residents lived in the city, and by the time of the 1980 census scarcely more than one-quarter of the SMSA population—27.6 percent—was found within the city limits.

---

3. *Detroit Free Press*, Republican Convention Special, 1980.

If suburbanization of jobs and amenities has provided the "pull" for Detroit's population loss, much of the "push" appears to have been caused by racial animosity. Detroit always has been a city of factory workers with few institutions of "high culture" (apart from a recently improved symphony orchestra and an excellent though little-attended Art Institute), but many of its homes are owner occupied (65 percent in 1976), producing strong attachments to neighborhood and ethnic culture. The large groups of Polish, Irish, German, Italian, and, more recently, Arab immigrants to Detroit have consistently used their relatively high wages to purchase houses in areas that have become homogeneous and culturally distinct. When southern whites were added to the earlier mix, and when large numbers of southern blacks appeared in the city during the early 1940s to take jobs in war production industries, racial tensions became impossible to control. Race riots occurred in 1943, in 1950, and again in 1967, when large portions of some city neighborhoods were burned down in a widely publicized "insurrection."[4]   Since that time the media repeatedly have reported incidents of interracial violence, often associated with the movement of black citizens into previously all-white neighborhoods.

Although media imagery may have magnified rather than simply reflected the realities of black-white tension, the realities clearly have contributed to a massive abandonment of the city by whites. A recent study by the Detroit Planning Department shows that nearly 400,000 whites left Detroit between 1960 and 1970, and it appears that another 300,000 white residents moved out between 1970 and 1977. A black population increase of nearly 100,000 during the sixties and 175,000 during the seventies has established Detroit as a predominantly black city. An estimated 57 percent of the city population was black in 1977, up from less than 30 percent in 1960, and the black proportion had grown even more by the time of the official 1980 census, when it stood at 63.1 percent.

The suburbs, meanwhile, have become both larger and whiter than before. As Detroit lost residents between 1960 and 1977, the rest of Wayne County (in which the city is located) gained 160,000 residents; Oakland County (northwest of the city) grew from 690,603 to 989,600 people; and Macomb County (northeast of the

---

4. For a useful analysis, see B. J. Widick, *Detroit, City of Race and Class Violence* (Chicago: Quadrangle Books, 1972).

city) increased its population from 407,230 to 684,100. A few blacks have trickled into some suburbs, mostly in Wayne County, but the proportion of blacks in Oakland County has remained steady at 3.5 percent, while the percentage of blacks in Macomb County actually declined from 1.7 to 1.6 percent between 1960 and 1970. White suburban growth often provides a stark contrast to the decline of Detroit. Sterling Heights in Macomb County grew from 14,622 residents in 1960 to an estimated 97,700 in 1977; Troy in Oakland County grew from 19,058 to 63,300 during the same period; Warren, also in Macomb County, grew from 63,343 to 169,300, of whom only 129 were black, in 1970. Black Detroit may be in decline, but its neighbors include a number of white suburban "boom towns."[5]

For the city, the economic implications of these population shifts are very severe indeed. The whites who have abandoned Detroit have been predominantly middle-income, educated, and taxpaying citizens. The city has been left with a population that is not only largely black, but also poorer, older, less well educated, and less able to generate either income or tax resources than its suburban counterparts. This does not mean that the average city family or household is poor in any absolute sense—far from it. Strong unions, effective bargaining tactics, and a traditionally productive dominant industry have combined to give many Detroiters reasonably high wages and fringe benefits, though the recent period of slow sales in the auto industry has led to the renegotiating of some union contract provisions. Detroit's mean family income of $18,077 ranked seventh among the nation's twenty largest metropolitan area central cities in 1977, while its median family income of $17,991 was exceeded then only by that of Anaheim, California. For the Detroit metropolitan area as a whole, however, mean family income was much higher, $22,641, suggesting a large discrepancy between city and suburban incomes.

The significance of this city-suburban difference becomes more clear when household rather than family income is compared. The 48 percent increase in median household income in Detroit between 1969 and 1977 did not match the considerably higher rate of increase for the SMSA (60 percent) or for the nation as a whole (62 percent). By 1977, median household income in

---

5. It should be noted that a number of older suburbs around Detroit are themselves losing population. Communities in the "first ring" like Ferndale or Royal Oak suffer from deterioration problems similar to those plaguing the city itself.

Detroit had fallen below the national level, and was more than $5,000 below the median for the SMSA. More than one-third of Detroit's residents, furthermore, had incomes of less than $7,000 in 1977, compared to no more than one-fifth for the SMSA and one-quarter for the nation as a whole. Although the proportion of Detroit households earning $20,000 or more is similar to the national proportion, suburban households are much better off: some 43 percent of suburban households earn $20,000 or more.

Detroit's position is thus somewhat paradoxical. Incomes in general are high, and a substantial fraction of the population is in the highest income class, but city incomes are not nearly so high as suburban incomes, and more than a third of the population has rather low incomes. Some 18 percent of the city's households were judged by the Planning Department to be in poverty in 1976-77, but the proportion in poverty was "especially high for blacks (24 percent), for female-headed households (37 percent), for single-parent families (44 percent), for young households where the head is eighteen to twenty-four (33 percent), for elderly households (20 percent), for widows (28 percent), and for house- holds receiving public assistance (64 percent)."[6] Another per- spective on data from the same study defines the context rather vividly by pointing out that 71 percent of poverty households in Detroit in 1976-77 were black. Not surprisingly, the Detroit SMSA consistently accounted for well over half of Michigan's AFDC caseload and two-thirds to four-fifths of the state's public assis- tance caseload during the 1970s, with most (80 percent) of these cases coming from the black poor of the city.

Part of the explanation for high levels of poverty and welfare caseloads in Detroit, of course, is the city's dependence on a single industry, which is itself extraordinarily sensitive to fluctuations in the national economy. Only five firms—Chrysler, GM, Budd, Uni- royal, and Massey-Ferguson—provided nearly 24 percent of the city's 425,000 jobs in 1977. All five are engaged in auto or truck manufacturing or related industries. Historically, even a moderate economic decline or a slight drop in auto sales has had a severe impact on the city. The 1974-75 recession caused national unem- ployment to rise from 5.6 percent to 8.5 percent; in Detroit, how- ever, unemployment was double the national figure, rising from 12.5 percent to 17.4 percent in 1975. Since that time the national recovery has been far stronger than the improvement in the city.

6. Detroit Planning Department, "Detroit Citizen Survey, 1976."

Indeed, throughout the decade of the 1970s unemployment in Detroit never fell below 8.3 percent and, at the end of the decade, in the midst of a serious "stagflation," it was again increasing, standing several points above the national rate. These estimates are conservative, since they count as unemployed only those receiving unemployment compensation or registered as job applicants, thus ignoring those who have dropped out of the labor force or are underemployed. These estimates also hide much higher rates of unemployment among specific groups. Black males between the ages of sixteen and twenty-four, particularly those who have dropped out of school, suffer unemployment rates estimated to be as high as 70 percent. Clearly Detroit has been and is a city of persistent unemployment, particularly among the young and the black.

In addition to the exaggerated impact of cyclical unemployment in a one-industry town, there is a deeper structural problem that afflicts the city. Although manufacturing and construction employment has been in decline, other sectors have been adding jobs in Detroit. Because of what city officials describe as "a basic mismatch of skills and available job openings," however, newly created jobs have little impact on unemployment. A Planning Department report states:

Many of Detroit's unemployed are blue-collar auto industry operatives who have become, over the years, what amounts to a surplus labor pool. The continued substitution of machinery for manpower has produced a large group of unemployed workers with few or no skills and little education beyond that required in an auto or auto-related occupation. On the other hand, the tremendous growth in the service industry over the past decade has opened up new jobs, but service jobs generally require an entirely different set of skills than those of industry. The transfer of workers from the manufacturing sector to the service sector cannot be accomplished, for the most part, without extensive retraining and education. . . . At the same time . . . the labor force now includes a significant group of youth from the "baby boom" years and increasing numbers of women. The auto industry as a major employer is adding new jobs, but the trend is in the "white collar" occupations. Youth, lacking basic education and work skills, cannot compete for the available jobs.[7]

Detroit thus faces not just periodic unemployment, but also the specter of a growing underclass of the permanently unemployed, forced to survive on welfare or other forms of assistance. The rapidity with which this underclass can grow is illustrated by the recent closing of Dodge Main, once the largest auto production

7. Detroit Planning Department, "Current Economic Situation, Detroit—January 1978" (mimeo), p. 2.

facility in the nation and the source of employment for nearly 5,000 workers, followed closely by a Uniroyal announcement that its Detroit tire plant would be shut down—and with it about 1,700 jobs. Some of these workers will be able to retire on pensions, but many presumably will fall into the surplus labor pool described above—unable to work in jobs that no longer exist, untrained for new jobs being created, and unprepared for premature retirement.

Unemployment not only contributes to increases in crime, mental disorders, and other signs of social disorganization,[8] but also generates a demand for governmental action even as it reduces the government's capacity to act. The largest local source of city revenue is the income tax; thus an increase in unemployment has a direct effect on the city's ability to function. Furthermore, because so many of the unemployed are black, stereotypical suburban images of a central city dominated by a large underclass of the black poor, seldom at work but always on welfare, are reinforced. It is not difficult to imagine how these images have contributed to the massive abandonment of the city by whites. Imagery aside, a major consequence of white flight and economic decline is a city with a highly *dependent* population and a diminishing capacity to meet the needs of that population.

Another major consequence of these trends is the very visible deterioration of the city's physical plant. Miles of storefronts along the neighborhood commercial strips have been boarded up. Whole neighborhoods have been turned into eyesores by large-scale residential abandonment—caused in many cases by poorly administered HUD mortgage programs. The dangers produced by large numbers of abandoned or boarded-up houses have prompted a massive city response: An average of more than 6,000 dwelling units have been demolished in the city in each of the past seven years. But Detroit is an old city. Nearly 56 percent of all residential and 42 percent of all nonresidential structures are more than fifty years old. Residential abandonment on the scale that has occurred thus means a continuing or growing need for demolition and reconstruction.

In the city's 1979-80 community development block grant (CDBG) application, for example, officials pointed out that a 1958 structure-by-structure survey produced an estimate "that it would

---

8. For some interesting evidence, see Harold M. Rose and Donald R. Deskins, Jr., "Felony Murder: The Case of Detroit," *Urban Geographic*, vol. 1, no. 1 (1980), pp. 1-21.

cost $1.2 billion to remove all known blighted buildings." The report admitted: "Today, the combined local resources of both the public and private sectors are inadequate to rapidly eliminate the blight that threatens many of our neighborhoods." Even if all blight were rapidly eliminated, the question of what to do with the cleared properties would remain. A recent survey of 45,000 residential plots on the east side of Detroit—some 10 percent of all assessable parcels in the city—discovered that 9,000 of these plots have come into city ownership.[9] Property tax delinquency has tripled in the past decade and exceeded 15 percent of the total tax levy in 1978. The city thus controls enough space in this one area alone to develop the equivalent of a "new city," housing 50,000 people or so. The financial investment required for such an undertaking, however, would be well beyond any resources likely to be available to the city. Financial resources required merely to keep up with necessary demolitions are already substantial, and demolition without redevelopment exaggerates the impression of a city in an advanced state of physical decline.

As it loses population and jobs, the city also loses capacity to generate tax revenue. The value of city real estate actually declined from $3.85 billion in 1961 to $3.77 billion in 1970. Large capital investments in downtown Detroit in the early 1970s—primarily the highly publicized Renaissance Center—increased real estate values somewhat, but by 1978 residential, commercial, and industrial property losses had brought equalized property values back down to $3.96 billion.[10] Nominal stability in property values, of course, indicates a considerable loss in "real" values, if inflation is taken into account; to keep up with the city's budget outlays, therefore, the tax rate has been steadily increased, from 44 mills in 1961, to 57 mills in 1971, and to 75 mills in 1978—by far the highest rate in Michigan.[11] In addition, a city income tax of 1 percent was adopted in 1962 and the rate was increased to 2 percent in 1968. (Nonresidents employed in the city pay only 0.5 percent on income.) But even these efforts to forestall deficits were not enough; city officials in 1970 imposed an "emergency" five-year utility tax (since re-enacted twice), increased charges and fees for various municipal services, and, as we shall see, began to lobby for more state and federal aid.

9. *Detroit Free Press*, December 11, 1977.
10. City of Detroit, *1978-79 Budget*, p. viii.
11. *Ibid.*, p. x.

Detroit Governance

Detroit is far and away the largest urban center in a state that,
like ancient Gaul, often seems divided into three separate and
very different parts: northern Michigan, western Michigan, and
Detroit or southeastern Michigan. These are three distinctively
different worlds. Northern Michigan includes the northern portion of Michigan's lower peninsula and the vast unpopulated for-
ests of the upper peninsula, joined together by the Mackinaw
Bridge. Tourism (including recreational hunting and fishing),
agriculture, and mining are the major industries in this area, which
includes no city larger than 25,000 in population and few municipalities larger than 5,000. Western Michigan includes resort towns
along the shores of Lake Michigan and the agricultural areas that
extend eastward from the lake. Michigan's second largest city,
Grand Rapids (197,000), is in this area, along with other moderately
large urban places such as Kalamazoo, Battle Creek, and Musk-
egon, each of which contains important industrial concentrations.
As a whole, western Michigan continues to be dominated by conservative political forces whose roots can be traced to fundamen-
talist religious beliefs associated with early Dutch and German
settlers of the area. Almost everything else of political significance
in Michigan lies within a forty-mile radius of Detroit: more than
half of the state's population, wealth, newspaper circulation, and,
of course, voters.

Detroit and southeastern Michigan are everything the rest of
the state is not: industrial, densely settled, culturally heterogene-
ous. Political encounters in Detroit take place not in the farm
bureau or legion hall, but in corporate boardrooms, country clubs,
union halls, churches, city halls—and often enough the streets.

These differences between Detroit and the rest of Michigan are
important because they define the context within which Detroit
interests are defined and debated in Lansing, the state capital. A
tradition of "good government" in Michigan, presumably a legacy
of early northern European and New England Yankee settlers, is
reflected today in a state administration that is highly professional-
ized, highly organized, and dominated by strong civil service
norms. These norms, together with the domination of statewide
elections by southeastern Michigan voters, encourage the executive branch to focus attention on the Detroit area. Within the state
legislature, however, more segmented areal representation
encourages a powerful regional consciousness that often leads to
conflict between Detroit and representatives of very different

regional interests. Detroit voters are predominantly Democrats and Democrats have controlled both houses of the legislature and filled all statewide offices except the governorship for the past decade. Benefits for Detroit are nonetheless difficult to obtain in the legislature. Republican Governor William G. Milliken, a moderate who needs support from southeastern Michigan to offset his own electoral weakness among more conservative upstate Republicans, has repeatedly shown a responsiveness to Detroit interests that sometimes contrasts sharply with legislative behavior. During Milliken's decade-long tenure, at least, party has been less important than position in structuring Lansing's response to Detroit's problems.

Detroit might have needed Governor Milliken's support less had it enjoyed more support from other governments in southeastern Michigan during the 1970s. Despite strong cultural and economic linkages, however, city and area interests have been defined very differently, to a considerable extent because area governance is so fragmented. Although Detroit is obviously the largest and most significant government in the region, 240 other governments exist in the counties of Wayne, Oakland, and Macomb alone, including eighty-six municipalities, forty-five townships, and eighty-nine school districts. Still another hundred governments are included in the three remaining counties of the Detroit SMSA. Because many of these governments have gained directly from Detroit's losses of people and jobs, it is not surprising that they have a view of municipal interest that differs from the Detroit view. Nor is it surprising, given the racial composition of the city and its surrounding suburbs, that these competing interests should occasionally be expressed in racial slurs of the harshest kind. Whatever they may have in common, Detroit and its neighboring governments remain divided by entrenched racial and economic barriers.

These barriers are strong enough to hinder development of major regional governing institutions. The Southeast Michigan Council of Governments (SEMCOG) is useful as an information-gathering agency, but it has no authority to provide other services and is weakened by the refusal of many area governments to participate as well as the resignation of some member governments from the organization. Without continued federal funding, in fact, its future existence would be in doubt. Although it is a city agency, the Detroit Water and Sewer Board is a true "regional" government, since it supplies water and sewer services to ninety-six suburban governments as well as the city itself. The city majority and the suburban minority on the Board of Water Commissioners frequently disagree over rates, however, occasionally filing well-publicized lawsuits that emphasize the extent to which even this cooperative activity is subject to city-suburban hostility.

The Southeast Michigan Transportation Authority (SEMTA) has made progress in coordinating suburban bus and rail transportation for the area and is chiefly responsible for planning an integrated city-suburban transit system to be funded by a $900 million federal grant. To date, suburban hostility to city plans for a subway component in the regional system and the city's desire to retain operational control over the city's own bus system have prevented final agreement. Legislative debate over an initial appropriation for a feasibility study, furthermore, has made clear that racial hostility remains an important source of suburban *and* city opposition to significant regional cooperation. Here, too, federal pressure has been and remains the strongest impetus to further action.

However fragmented area governance may be, the city's own government seems both coherent and coordinated. The Board of Education, an independent school district, is the only major government other than the municipal government operating wholly within the city. Only a few special districts exist to confuse responsibility for services, and Detroit's "reformed" institutions are easily comprehended. Elections are officially nonpartisan, with a mayor and nine city council members elected at large for four-year terms. Because of the strong civil service tradition, the mayor's appointment powers are limited, but the mayor controls the budget and, as we shall see, there are ways for a politically powerful mayor to enhance his appointment opportunities.[12] Election of the nine city council members at large, rather than by ward, gives each of them considerable prominence, which is further enhanced by the high salaries ($40,000) and constant sessions associated with one of the nation's few full-time municipal legislative bodies. The city's main governing institutions, therefore, are visible, coherently organized, and well staffed.

An informal structure of influence is also apparent in Detroit. Because the Detroit economy is so concentrated, leaders of a few industries, banks, and law firms—including various vice-presi-

12. The new city charter adopted in 1974 vastly increased the number of positions open to mayoral appointment.

dents or directors of civic or governmental affairs—make up an economic elite that, because it is relatively small, is easily consulted on matters of major public concern. To some extent these interactions are formalized. The Metropolitan Fund organizes periodic meetings that bring most members of this elite together with political and governmental leaders, and the Citizens Research Council of Michigan provides a research and analysis capacity. Action-oriented projects typically are funneled through organizations such as the Central Business District Association, Detroit Renaissance, or New Detroit, Inc. But the economic elite is small enough, and its members familiar enough with each other, that formal actions are seldom necessary. If major concerted effort is deemed desirable, informal communication among leaders is sufficient.

Labor influence in Detroit is similarly concentrated. Bitter and often violent struggles to organize the automobile industry in the 1930s created widespread sympathy and support for labor interests among the largely working-class population of the city. Detroit is now a strong union town in which the United Automobile Workers union exercises continuous and comprehensive political influence, from the definition of issues to the selection of candidates to the conduct of campaigns—almost always for Democratic party candidates. The recent election of UAW President Douglas Fraser to the board of the Chrysler Corporation extends a union tradition of innovation in labor-management relations that has helped to make the UAW an extremely powerful organization statewide, as well as in the city. Although less innovative, the Teamsters union also plays a powerful role in the city and state politics, relying on a large and aggressive local membership. The city's emergent public employee unions—police and fire, municipal workers, and the teachers—have become more aggressive, effectively using work stoppages or threats of work stoppages to win higher benefits. These and several other less visible union organizations occasionally coordinate their actions through the Metropolitan Labor Council.

Detroit's two major newspapers, the liberal *Free Press* and the conservative *News*, are also significant actors in the city's political environment. A lively competition for increased circulation encourages aggressive local reporting that repeatedly affects the city's political agenda. Reformed governmental institutions, moreover, permit the *Free Press* and the *News* to exert considerable electoral influence as well. Because elections are nonpartisan and citywide, Detroit voters lack party labels or ward identity to help them determine their electoral preferences. With dozens of names on the ballot (recall that all city officers, including the nine city council members, are elected together), preference determination is no easy task for the typical voter who is not especially active in politics. Both papers devote a great deal of attention to endorsements, publishing their lists of preferred candidates on election day for voters to take with them into polling places. These political activities have proven to be quite influential and candidates accordingly do as much as they can to win newspaper endorsement.[13]

Detroit's concentrated and highly organized institutional structure produces a small group of elite leaders who easily exchange information and opinions among themselves. Interviews with ninety-two members of this elite in mid-1975 revealed that most of them (63 percent) spend half or more of their time working on public issues, bringing to such issues attitudes that are largely pragmatic rather than doctrinaire or ideological. For example, most (71 percent) of these leaders are supportive of new initiatives to deal with city problems and virtually all (85 percent) favor public or some mix of public and private sector actions, rather than private solutions alone. Members of the Detroit elite also have a broad view of the appropriate functions of city governments. A large majority rejects the notion that cities should stick to basic services such as police, fire, and streets; similarly large majorities affirm the obligation of cities to provide not only shopping facilities and parks, but cultural activities, housing for the poor, and clean neighborhood environments as well.[14]   These views were an important part of the setting in which Detroit's newly elected black mayor would operate.

By the time Coleman A. Young assumed office as mayor in January 1974, the city was well on the way toward what the mayor was to call in 1977 "the worst budget crisis in Detroit since the 1930s." A rapidly developing recession was producing drastic increases in unemployment, along with related problems of welfare and crime. A year later, in February 1975, unemployment had exceeded 22 percent and remained at this high level throughout 1975, never

13. For an analysis of the impact of newspaper endorsements on electoral outcomes in Detroit, see Steven L. Coombs, "Editorial Endorsements and Electoral Outcomes" (Ph.D. dissertation, University of Michigan, 1978).

14. This summary is derived from the 1975 Detroit Area Study, which I conducted in cooperation with Bruce Bowen.

falling below a monthly rate of 17.3 percent. The effect on city services was severe. More than 4,000 city employees were laid off during 1975, a hiring freeze was instituted, and museums and recreation centers were shut down or forced to operate on sharply reduced schedules. Despite these efforts, the city's financial condition did not improve and Mayor Young could not avoid a pessimistic projection in his January 1976 state of the city message:

The cost of city government this year will be about $810 million. That's almost $50 million more than we will receive in revenues. Not because our spending got out of control, by the way. It's because state and federal revenue sharing fell $12 million short, because Blue Cross insurance jumped $4 million, because new tax programs were never enacted in the state legislature, and because you can't tax people who are out of work—and our own income tax collections dropped $6 million. . . . Sometime in March, just to meet the payroll, the city of Detroit will have to borrow $64 million. That's three times as much money as we've ever borrowed before. . . . On July 1, already $50 million in deficit and with borrowing at record levels, the city faces an immediate obligation to be paying $50 million more in pay increases, cost of living allowances, and fringe benefits for city employees. . . . No amount of layoffs, or of cutbacks in services, can enable us to meet this combined $100 million deficit—and the millions more that will be added by continued inflation.

As the national economy improved during 1976 the city's unemployment rate fell, improving its fiscal position somewhat. That improvement, coupled with increasing state and federal aid during 1976 and 1977, enabled the city to weather this $100 million crisis and gradually restore the laid-off workers to the payroll. By midsummer of 1978, however, it had become clear that another $100 million deficit was in the making, partly as a result of arbitration awards to the city's police and fire unions that imposed an additional $50 million burden on the city's wage bill. Detroit police and firefighters, among the highest paid in the nation, are well organized and politically powerful in a strong union city. The city took what the mayor described as these "lavish awards" to court, but the Michigan Supreme Court upheld the awards in mid-1980. In the meantime, layoffs began again in late 1978 and another hiring freeze was imposed. In presenting the 1979-80 budget, moreover, the mayor was forced to admit that the legally required "balance" between revenues and expenditures had been achieved only by resorting to some "very highly optimistic assumptions about the future." As he put it in his budget message,

We do have a balanced budget, to be sure. But it is a budget balanced with $40 million of revenue items which will require action by either the state or federal legislatures and to that extent are entirely beyond our control.

Detroit government thus has been delicately balanced between fiscal collapse and organizational survival. Plagued by massive population losses, degeneration of its tax base, and a revenue structure highly sensitive to national economic conditions, yet confronted with the needs of a population that is increasingly dependent on government services, the city has lost much of its fiscal capacity to support local services. Massive reinvestment in the city to create more factories, commercial centers, and residential areas is the only hope of rebuilding both the property and income tax bases, but massive redevelopment can happen only in the long run, if at all. In the short run, locally generated taxes, assessed at four times the statewide average,[15] support a declining share of annual city expenditures. In Detroit, traditional sources of city revenue are running dry.

15. This refers to the relative tax effort used for state of Michigan revenue sharing distribution and includes the millage equivalents of revenues generated by the local income and utility taxes as well as property taxes.

2. Federal Aid, Fiscal 1978

The problem of finding adequate revenues has hardly been a secret from city officials, many of whom have provided leadership in finding solutions. Former Mayor Jerome P. Cavanagh, for example, helped to originate the "model cities" plan that became national policy in the mid-1960s, working closely with Walter Reuther, then head of the UAW. Cavanagh and his successors, Roman Gribbs and Coleman Young, also have invested considerable effort in seeking higher levels of assistance from the state government. One result of these efforts is a city government populated by individuals and organizational units skilled in generating outside funding. The city's success at meeting this "external imperative" is summarized in table 1, which compares local, state, and federal contributions to city revenues for fiscal 1975 through fiscal 1978. Local sources increased by barely 22 percent during that period, while federal aid jumped by 62 percent. Even more striking is the doubling of state government assistance that occurred in just four years. By 1978 federal aid accounted for 24 percent and state aid produced more than 17 percent of all revenue available to the city.

Although these increases in outside support sometimes have been attributed entirely to Mayor Young's political skills, their sources are considerably more complex. The largest annual increments in federal aid occurred in fiscal 1976, when nearly $60 million was added, and in fiscal 1975, when $28 million was added. These increments were derived from two programs that originated in Washington rather than Detroit—CETA and transportation aid. These programs were congressional initiatives, implemented during the tenure of a Republican administration not perceived to be enthusiastic about providing aid to large cities.

Nor does it appear that Mayor Young affected the structure of federal aid to Detroit very much during this period. General revenue sharing was already in place when he assumed office, the CETA and transportation increments stabilized after the 1976 increments that were decided in Washington, and the shift from urban renewal to the community development block grant program was also in the process of being decided in Washington. The only substantial addition to federal assistance to affect Detroit after 1976 was the countercyclical program, which generated $17 and $23 million respectively in 1977 and 1978. The mayor lobbied hard for these funds in Washington, as he did for other federal initiatives such as the local public works program, but a great many other people in city nonprofit and regional agencies were equally active in generating federal money. This point is worth emphasizing less to minimize the mayor's role than to clarify it. The mayor was one among many seeking federal aid; only the mayor, however, could build and coordinate the coalitions required to be successful in that search.

Shortly after his election, Mayor Young and his closest staff associates decided to put together a plan for dealing with the city's unemployment problem, which was moving from "serious" to "critical" as 1974 came to an end. The strategy was to present the plan in Washington with as much unified local support behind it as could be mustered. As city bureaucrats began putting the plan together, the mayor was organizing a coalition of commercial, industrial, labor, and civic leaders. In April 1975 members of this coalition journeyed to Washington to present a "Moving Detroit Forward" plan to President Gerald Ford and members of his cabinet. One participant later remembered this meeting as one in which "all the weight was on our side of the table." The presidents of the major automobile corporations were there; Governor Milliken, a close political ally of President Ford was there; Max Fisher, a major Republican fund raiser and close ally of President Ford was there; members of the Michigan congressional delegation and other political leaders were there. It was obviously a gathering that represented all segments of the city, put together with a view toward the coming presidential election as well as the city's needs. Although the meeting produced little immediate result, it did stimulate a commitment from President Ford to reserve $600 million in federal funds for the construction of a Detroit subway. However symbolic this "commitment" may have been—five years later nothing more than agreement to perform an

Table 1. *Federal, State, and Total Revenues, Fiscal Years 1975–78*
(dollars in millions)

Source	1975		1976		1977		1978	
	Amount	Percentage	Amount	Percentage	Amount	Percentage	Amount	Percentage
Federal	$173.6	20.7	$232.1	25.4	$ 255.5	24.7	$ 279.7	24.0
State	100.2	12.0	116.4	12.7	173.8	16.8	201.9	17.3
Subtotal	273.8	32.7	348.5	38.1	429.3	41.5	481.6	41.3
Local	562.8	67.3	565.2	61.9	603.1	58.5	683.6	58.7
Grand total	838.6	100.0	913.7	100.0	1,032.4	100.0	1,165.2	100.0

Source: Annual financial reports, various years.

engineering study has been achieved—it did suggest the potential power of Young's coalition-building activities.

Federal aid to Detroit increased substantially in 1976, as noted earlier, but Mayor Young clearly viewed President Ford as a hindrance rather than a help and decided to work against his election. "We had to establish a new relationship with the federal government," the mayor said later, "to replace one that had complete and callous disregard for the Detroits of this nation—whether the president was from San Clemente or from Grand Rapids."[1]   Young was a strong and, more importantly, an early supporter of Jimmy Carter. When Carter was elected, Young became someone whose voice counted in Washington. Detroit's legal counsel in Washington became an assistant secretary of transportation; the city finance director assumed a senior position in the Office of Management and Budget; another close associate of the mayor became treasury undersecretary, and another became a senior official at the Department of Housing and Urban Development. With the new administration, therefore, the mayor was able to establish a network of high-level officials to complement his already close congressional relationships. Along with his strong leadership coalition in Detroit, his network of ties to city neighborhood groups, and a bureaucracy that could produce when necessary, the mayor seemed well on the way to having it all "together."

A "together" mayor has in fact had tangible consequences for Detroit—whether or not he can claim much credit for having brought home more "bacon" than anyone else. Two examples can make the point. In 1976 the mayor learned from congressional sources that an emergency public works program would almost certainly be passed and organized a crash program for city officials to develop project applications. When the program was approved by President Ford the city was ready with $132 million in project proposals, of which some $22.4 million were approved—the fourth-highest city allocation in the country (after New York, Los Angeles, and Chicago) and the largest allocation per unemployed person in the country. A few months later the newly elected Democratic president added another $4 billion to the program and again Detroit was ready, this time receiving approval for an additional twelve grants totaling $23.8 million, including a $5 million grant to help renovate Tiger Stadium. Whether or not Detroit

_____

1. Mayor Coleman A. Young, "State of the City Message," January 31, 1977, p. 4.

would have received less in local public works money had the mayor not been paying attention is impossible to say; what is clear is that the mayor was on his toes, the bureaucracy turned out the necessary paperwork, and more than $46 million was received.

The second example involves the mayor's ability to protect the city from federal efforts to determine how federal funds should be used. In principle, CETA was a program designed to move unemployed workers back into the labor market by providing job training for people lacking marketable skills. Although the program was ideally suited for a city in which large numbers of workers have become permanently unemployed, the city's short-run fiscal problems have been so severe that most of the city's CETA funds have been used to rehire city workers (especially police) who had been temporarily laid off. In April 1976 the Chicago regional office of the Department of Labor refused to allow Detroit to use more than 10 percent of its CETA allocation to rehire city employees. The city went to court to challenge this ruling, but when court action failed the mayor took his case directly to the president. Using Max Fisher as an intermediary, the mayor was able to persuade President Ford to intervene by voiding the ruling made in the Chicago regional office and by transferring the Labor Department official who had made the ruling. Two years later, legislation enacted under a Democratic administration set maximum salary and participation limits for CETA-funded employees that would have forced Detroit to lay off as many as 2,400 employees. Again the mayor lobbied hard in Washington, this time for a waiver of the new regulations, and again he was successful. Although the city has done little training with its CETA funds, and the ranks of the structurally unemployed continue to grow, the city government has at least been saved from mass layoffs or massive deficits or both.

The results of these efforts by the mayor and his coworkers can be seen clearly in table 2, which reports federal funds available to and spent by the city in fiscal 1978. This table also reports federal funds available to and spent by the Detroit School District, which is independent of the city government but another major user of federal dollars. These numbers are conservative estimates. Allocations for health grants are not reported, for example, although it is probable that half or more of the $15 million in state grants for health originate in Washington. Nor do we show here an $8 million, first-round grant to Wayne State University, expendable in Detroit but allocated to Lansing by the Economic Development

Table 2. *Federal Funds to Detroit and Overlying Governments, Fiscal Year 1978*
(thousands of dollars)

Category	Carryover from previous years	Fiscal year 1978 funds	Total federal aid available	Expenditures in 1978	Carryover to fiscal 1979
		CITY OF DETROIT			
Operating					
Antirecession fiscal assistance	0	23,212	23,212	23,212	0
CETA titles I, III, STIP	4,139	29,097	30,236	28,401	1,835
Community development block grants[a]	3,893	5,581	9,473	8,586	2,571
Health grants[b]	—	—	—	—	—
General revenue sharing	0	40,246	40,246	40,246	0
Housing rent subsidy	0	5,272	5,272	5,272	0
Law Enforcement Assistance Admin.	3,977	1,101	5,079	3,314	1,764
Older Americans	0	16,837	16,837	16,837	0
CETA titles II, VI—PSE	56,939	0[c]	56,939	48,198	8,740
Urban mass transit (via SEMTA)	0	16,837	16,837	16,837	0
Subtotal, operating	—	—	—	193,062	—
Capital					
Community development block grants	13,032	18,683	31,715	22,050	8,609
Environmental Protection Agency	64,927	22,811	87,739	27,212	60,527
Local public works	16,558	23,790	40,348	9,706	30,642
Urban Mass Transp. Admin.[d]	0	6,861	6,861	6,861	0
Urban renewal	20,375	0	20,375	9,987	10,388

Subtotal, capital	—	—	—	75,817	—
Total, City of Detroit	—	—	—	268,879	—

DETROIT PUBLIC SCHOOLS

Operating					
Elementary & Secondary Education Act	0	26,316	26,316	26,316	0
Food service programs	0	16,110	16,110	16,110	0
Emergency School Aid Act	0	8,548	8,548	8,548	0
Public service employment[e]	0	12,764	12,764	12,764	0
Other	0	7,063	7,063	7,063	0
Subtotal, operating	—	—	—	70,802	—
Capital					
Assorted federal aid	430	1,500	1,930	1,719	211
Total, Detroit public schools	—	—	—	72,520	—

a. CDBG is reported by the city as a total. The figures are split between capital (77 percent) and operating (23 percent) based on actual department experience.

b. The city received about $15 million in a series of health grants from the state, perhaps 50 percent of which was federal pass-through.

c. The city received an eighteen-month allocation in fiscal 1977 that carried into 1978.

d. UMTA capital amount is 80 percent of the reported grants figure of $8,576,153, because the state matching share is 20 percent.

e. Received from the city of Detroit as prime sponsor.

Administration. Even without these sums Detroit had close to $400 million in federal aid available in fiscal 1978, and spent nearly $270 million. The amount spent is more than twice the amount contributed to the city's general fund by the income tax ($133 million), nearly two-and-one-half times the $114 million in general fund revenues realized from all property taxes in 1978, and nearly equal to the $282 million Detroit raised in 1978 from *all* local sources—property, income, and utility taxes; special assessments; and all other taxes and tax penalties. To generate that amount of additional revenue from local sources the income tax would have to be doubled, or the property tax rate increased by more than 62 percent. Detroit's problems are obviously large, but this is just as obviously a large federal response.

The federal contribution is even more impressive when federal aid to other governments operating in Detroit is taken into account. More than $72.5 million in federal money was spent by the school district in 1978, including some $12.7 million in CETA funds transferred from the city government. Federal sums spent by Wayne County, SEMTA, and SEMCOG in Detroit are estimated in table 3. These figures, too, are conservative estimates, because county spending within Detroit is calculated as a function of Detroit's share of county population and many federal programs operated by the county are known to spend disproportionate sums in the city. Thus, while table 3 reports about $345.7 million, federal grant expenditures by governments operating in Detroit in 1978 were almost certainly much higher. If Hamtramck and Highland Park, two municipalities that lie wholly within the boundaries of Detroit, were taken into account, a better estimate of federal outlays within the city would be closer to $400 million.

It is important to note that more than 70 percent of federal funds spent by the city and nearly all of the federal dollars spent by the school district supported program operations rather than capital projects. Much of this support comes with few or no strings attached. General revenue sharing and ARFA together provided more than $63 million for the city to do with essentially as the city saw fit. Other grants must be spent on defined functions. Urban mass transit support must go to the Detroit bus system and Older Americans funds must be spent on the city's neighborhood centers, for example, but the city remains free to develop its own programs within those functional areas.

Grants for capital projects clearly are more "bound" to a specific structure or system of structures but here, too, the city decides

Table 3. *Estimated Expenditures from Federal Sources,*
Detroit and Related Governments, Fiscal 1978

Government	Amount
City of Detroit Operating and capital	$268,879,494
School District of Detroit Operating and capital (less PSE received from the city)	59,755,839
Southeastern Michigan Transportation Authority Operating and capital	—[a]
Wayne County Operating and capital	16,116,872[b]
Southeastern Michigan Council of Governments Operating and capital	910,816[c]
Total	$345,663,021

a. According to SEMTA, all city expenditures are via DOT.

b. Wayne County, which spent about $56 million in federal money during 1977, has yet to publish a financial report for 1978. Its books were termed unauditable by the Michigan Auditor General's Office. An improved reporting system is anticipated. Based on 1977 figures, the $56 million, less CETA and block grant funds of $25,705,127, could be thought of as spent 53.2 percent within the city, because 53.2 percent of Wayne's population lives in the city. This could be calculated as $56,000,000 less $25,705,127, equaling $30,294,873 x 0.532, or $16,116,872 expended in the city of Detroit.

c. In 1978, the Southeastern Michigan Council of Governments, an eight-county planning consortium, spent a total of $3,903,638, of which 86 percent was federally supplied. That figure, $3,318,092, on a population basis, could be thought of as being 27.45 percent expended in the city, which amounts to $910,816.

what projects to propose for the local public works program, or for CDBG. Although these dollars come from outside, city agencies decide how to use them.

One final point of interest is the considerable amount of available operating support that was *not* used by the city in 1978. Nearly $9 million in PSE money and close to $2 million in CETA dollars were not used in a city whose main problem for years has been both cyclical and structural unemployment, and whose year-end fiscal balance has been negative for much of the past decade. This is an important as well as an interesting point, to which we will return.

Table 4. *Detroit's Revenues from State, Fiscal Years 1975–78*
(thousands of dollars)

City Fund and Source	1975	1976	1977	1978
General Fund				
State income tax	24,792	24,366	30,107	40,348
State intangibles tax	10,812	17,682	1,649	1,649
Liquor and beer licenses	993	968	856	848
State sales tax	23,698	25,424	28,813	32,884
Single business tax	0	25,424	2,814	32,884
Grants—health	6,792	14,797	12,660	14,990
Cultural reimbursement	0	0	4,202	5,091
Library Fund				
State grants	972	861	748	575
Cultural reimbursement	0	0	5,500	6,500
Shared taxes	0	0	453	460
Neighborhood Services Fund				
Michigan Labor Dept.	0	484	358	1,729
Street Funds				
Major streets				
gas & weight	19,412	19,605	20,223	21,188
State grants	0	150	25	35
Local streets				
gas & weight	5,338	5,392	5,570	5,817
Hospital Fund				
State contribution	0	0	8,000	0
Transportation Fund				
State via SEMTA	6,442	4,594	16,278	22,470
State capital outlay	0	12	42	50
Trolley project	0	417	1,361	51
State share of				
federal capital outlay				
via SEMTA	910	1,684	568	1,715
Total revenue from state	100,162	116,436	173,786	201,914
Total revenue,				
all sources	836,560	913,742	1,032,400	1,165,214
Memorandum:				
State funds as a				
percentage of total	11.97	12.74	16.83	17.33

Source: City financial reports, 1978–79.

State financial assistance to Detroit in 1978 totaled $202 million, considerably less than the $270 million in federal aid, but state aid had more than doubled between 1975 and 1978. Much of this increase was a result of Michigan's new single business tax, effective in fiscal 1977, coupled with Michigan's older tradition of sharing state-collected income, sales, and gasoline taxes with local governments. As table 4 shows, however, substantial increases have occurred for activities labeled cultural reimbursement, transportation, and even a one-time grant for a hospital contribution. These changes reflect the mayor's energy to some extent, but even more they reflect Governor William G. Milliken's strong commitment to urban areas and his willingness to demonstrate that commitment with funds for Detroit.

Milliken's urban commitment was evident as far back as 1971, when he approved a major revision of the state's revenue sharing program that doubled Detroit's revenue from the program. At the same time, Milliken approved a special one-time grant of $5 million for Detroit as compensation for revenues lost as a result of the 1970 census. Detroit experienced another 44 percent increment in state revenues as a consequence of the 1975 single business tax, and in 1976 Milliken proposed that a tax base sharing plan be adopted for southeastern Michigan. Revenues generated as a result of increased commercial and industrial development were to be shared by all seven counties in the region, instead of accruing only to the local and county jurisdiction in which the development was located. Detroit obviously would have benefited from this plan, but suburban opposition defeated it. The governor had at least raised the issue, demonstrating his interest in seeking innovative solutions as well as providing fiscal assistance. Milliken also had agreed to join Mayor Young in leading the delegation to Washington to plead the city's case before President Ford, and in fact had taken the lead in establishing the political and social contacts necessary for that visit. Milliken, in short, was both sympathetic to the city's problems and actively engaged in seeking solutions.

The failure of the Washington visit to produce immediate results implied that the mayor, like his predecessors, would have to press the city's case even harder at the state level. For years city spokesmen had argued that Detroit provided facilities used by people from all over the region and state, no less than by the city itself, and that equity required that taxpayers from across the region and state contribute to the support of those facilities. These

Table 5. *Appropriations for Programs in Equity Package,*
Fiscal 1977—80
(thousands of dollars)

	1977	1978	1979	1980
Library	5,500	6,500	6,500	7,500
Institute of Art	3,300	4,349	7,100	10,300
History museum	700	742	742	1,742
General hospital	8,000	—	—	—
Pension subsidy	9,200	9,200	9,200	9,200
Health labs	600	—	—	—
Total	27,300	20,801	23,542	28,742

Source: *Annual Financial Report, City of Detroit, Michigan, 1978–79.*

arguments had seldom produced major change, but in the spring of
1976, after a great deal of public as well as private wrangling, Milliken and Young agreed to submit two bills to the legislature. The
first authorized Detroit to levy a three-mill tax on property owners
to provide $15 million for refuse collection and disposal. The sec-
ond bill appropriated $27.8 million for a "state equity package"
containing funds for specific institutional support. As finally
passed, this package included $5.5 million for the Detroit Main
Library, $3.3 million for the Detroit Institute of Art, $700,000 for
the Detroit Historical Museum, $600,000 for the city's health labo-
ratories, $8 million for the Detroit General Hospital, and $9.2 million for the unfunded pension costs of the transportation
department. Later that year, after a particularly brutal crime on a
Detroit freeway, the state assumed responsibility for patrolling the
freeways around Detroit. This relieved the city of some $5 million
in costs.

Table 5, which shows the "equity package" appropriations
since 1976, suggests that the package has become institutional-
ized. The hospital and health labs funds were one-time grants, but
the library, art institute, and historical museum grants have
increased, and the pension subsidy continues. One result of this
funding breakthrough has been a more-or-less continuous debate
over the desirability of transferring funding for other activities to
the state; the zoo has been a focal point, as the courts have been.
In the meantime, another urban grants bill was passed in 1978; a
bill to provide funds to compensate for losses due to the 1980 census is under debate at this writing (summer 1980), and the city is
again laying off employees and facing another recession-induced

Table 6. *Federally Supported and Total Positions,
Five Common Services, 1978*

Agency	Federally supported positions	Total positions	Percentage federal
Police	690	6,558	11
Fire	198	1,854	11
Environmental protection	517	2,582	20
Parks and recreation	427	1,501	28
General administration	447	2,866	16

Source: Author's calculations.

deficit of even larger proportions. The state clearly has assumed a major funding role, in a way that suggests the possibility of major changes in the assignment of government responsibilities for the Detroit area. In this sense the growth of state assistance has a significance far beyond the dollar increments.

The Dependence Issue

At one level, Detroit has been extraordinarily successful in managing its fiscal problem. Despite serious erosion of the income and property tax base, the city has maintained services by shifting an increasing fraction of the costs of those services to the state and federal governments. This should not be taken to mean that the level of services maintained is similar to what it had been. On the contrary, in most cases service levels have declined. Ridership on city buses declined from 115.2 million trip-fares in fiscal 1970 to 77.8 million in 1979; trash collectors covered 50 percent fewer routes in 1979 than in 1973; firefighters on duty at any given time declined from 425 in 1973 to 340 in 1979; three of the twenty-nine branches of the public library operating in 1973 have been closed, and the system closes two branches per month on a rotating basis to conserve funds. Large doses of federal and state aid, in other words, have done little more than prevent the far worse deterioration in city services that would have occurred without those outside dollars.

Does this mean that Detroit has become dependent on outside aid for its continued existence? Or, since federal aid is the largest component of outside support for Detroit, is the city now so "hooked" on federal grants that any significant reduction in such funds would cause serious disruption of city operations? Answers to these questions are less obvious than they may appear, in part because dollar totals are subject to a variety of interpretations. One interpretation that seems helpful is to compare federal funds to local revenue sources. Doing so allows us to develop the concept of "replacement ratio," that is, the extent to which local revenues would have to be increased in order to replace federal dollars if such dollars became unavailable.

If all local sources of general revenue (fees and charges as well as taxes) are included in the calculation, a 38.8 percent increase in such revenues would have been required to equal federal operating grants in 1978. If only tax revenue is considered, a 57.4 percent increase in such revenue would have been required to match operating grants, and a 63.5 percent boost in local taxes would have been needed to replace both operating and capital grants taken together. Viewed this way, Detroit's fiscal dependence on federal aid was quite massive in 1978.

Federal grants supported all of the positions budgeted in 1978 for the Departments of Neighborhood Services, Manpower, and Planning, and a large fraction of Health Department positions. Positions supported by CETA funds were spread through thirty-seven of the city's forty-five major operating agencies. The number of federally supported positions ranged from 11 to 28 percent of total positions for five common municipal functions (see table 6). While parks and environmental care (streets, sanitation) were more heavily dependent on federally supported positions than were police, fire, or general administration, federal funding was important for all of these basic city activities. These basic services were no longer being delivered as extensively as they once were, but they were still being delivered, in no small measure because of federal aid. In Detroit, fiscal dependence is so huge that it implies a service dependence as well.

Fiscal dependence does not appear to carry with it a similar degree of federal control over how federal money is to be used, however. Roughly 70 percent of all federal assistance is used as general support, with federal constraints applied loosely or not at all, or functional support, to which only vaguely defined functional constraints are attached. The city maintains separate accounts for the CDBG program and a few minor health programs, but manages all remaining federal funds through a single master account from which funds are drawn as needed for various federally supported activities. Periodic audit and reporting requirements must be met, of course, but the city otherwise has considerable leeway in controlling the flow of federal dollars through city agencies. Capital grants are more bound to designated projects, but the city designates the projects for which it will apply, and allocates federal funds to them according to its own priorities rather than those of the federal government. In Detroit, a high level of fiscal dependence on federal aid does not imply programmatic dependence. Indeed, when we consider what the condition of the city treasury might be without the present level of federal support, it seems clear that federal aid has made possible a variety of local program initiatives that otherwise would have been no more than dreams.

3. Employment Effects

To conclude that external assistance has been used primarily to help maintain existing city services is also to conclude that such assistance has enabled the city to retain municipal jobs that might otherwise have been lost. In the mid-1950s the city had more than 29,000 employees; by the mid-1970s average annual city employment had shrunk to roughly 25,000. This is not an insignificant loss, but considering the massive losses of population and tax base that occurred during this period, job shrinkage could have been far worse.

Part of the reason that more city jobs were not eliminated has been the strong mutuality of interest between city agencies, reluctant to abandon established service commitments, and municipal employee unions, reluctant to lose jobs. This mutuality of interest, coupled with increasing militance on the part of union leaders faced with an apparently continuous budget "crisis," has achieved very favorable results for city workers. Wage contracts for city employees now routinely include not only high wages and fringe benefits but cost-of-living adjustments as well, imposing significant cost increases on the city even without increases in the number of workers. In fiscal 1978 the compensation package for city workers averaged $28,000 per employee, of which $12,000 was for fringe benefits, while the average expenditure for police officers and firefighters exceeded $46,000, including some $21,000 in fringes. According to one recent study, these provisions have made public employment in Detroit superior to typical employment conditions in the private sector.[1] Economic and social con-

---

1. Citizens Research Council, "City of Detroit Salaries: A Comparison" (Council Comments No, 912, June 5, 1980, processed).

ditions in the city have seriously decayed, and some jobs have been lost, but remaining city employees have become increasingly well paid and well cared for.

Using data on funds available, we estimate that about 27 percent of all city employees were supported by federal funds, and another 19 percent by state funds in fiscal 1978. These estimates assume average compensation of $28,000 per employee. They also assume that, apart from the specifically budgeted positions, 70 percent of outside funds are allocated to wages and fringes, in keeping with the general distribution of wages and other costs in the city budget. The estimates may also be conservative, since they are based on 25,313 budgeted positions rather than the average of about 24,500 in actual employment. Although necessarily imprecise, these estimates do suggest the remarkable extent to which Detroit has come to rely on state and federal dollars to support its employees. Without external funding in 1978, the city would have been forced to either reduce its work force by nearly half or to drastically lower then-current levels of wages and fringe benefits, or both.

Table 7 permits us to observe the program impacts of federal dollars that can be specifically traced to departmental budgets. Project grants for health, for programs for the aged operated by the neighborhood services departments, and for planning are concentrated in a few departments, but PSE funds provide substantial support for most city agencies. Taken together, these federal dollars were used in 1978 to support virtually all city activities; only seven of the forty-five agencies budgeted no federally supported positions in that year.

The figures shown in table 7 are for only those federal dollars that can be traced to particular departments. An additional 3,046 positions were suppported by federal dollars that the city placed in its general fund, in effect merging them with locally raised revenues. If these positions were used for basic services in the same proportion as the positions shown in table 7, the impact of federal funds on total city operations would be much more dramatic.

The extent to which federal funds support basic services is an important point precisely because most federal funds are either intended to be or become general support dollars. Only 1,000 or so federally supported positions are tied to specific federal programs, primarily in health and aging services. These positions are extremely vulnerable to federal program change or cancellation but, by the same token, they are far less vulnerable to changes in

Table 7. Summary of Positions Budgeted, Fiscal 1978, by Funding Source

Department	Gen. fund	CETA	Other[a]	Total
Airport	15	8	0	23
Fine Arts	143	0	0	143
Budget	38	6	0	44
Bldgs. and Safety	300	25	1	326
Civic Center	86	26	0	112
Comm. and Econ. Dev.	284	11	0	295
Consumers Affairs	38	3	0	41
Corrections	181	0	0	181
Council of the Arts	4	16	2	22
Data Processing	161	15	0	176
Environ. Protection and Maintenance	2,065	509	8	2,582
Finance	463	83	11	557
Fire	1,656	198	0	1,854
Health	663	103	397	1,163
Historical	44	28	0	72
Hospital	1,509	28	0	1,537
Housing	504	16	7	52
Human Rights	26	7	0	33
Law	104	3	0	107
Manpower	0	219	1	220
Mayor's Office	89	33	0	122
Municipal Parks	72	49	0	121
Neighborhood Services	0	4	442	446
Personnel	98	85	1	184
Planning	0	13	56	69
Police	5,868	650	40	6,558
Public Information	42	7	0	49
Public Lighting	1,002	339	39	1,380
Recreation	1,002	339	39	1,380
Senior Citizen	7	2	1	10
Transportation	2,157	9	0	2,166
Water and Sewer	2,231	16	0	2,247
Zoo	187	15	0	202
Auditor General	44	1	0	45
City Clerk	23	0	0	23
City Council	43	1	0	44
City Planning	6	0	4	10
Election Commission	83	8	0	91
Ombudsman	11	0	0	11
Zoning Board of Appeals	16	2	0	18
Recorder's Ct.—Criminal	110	0	0	110
Recorder's Ct.—Jury	6	0	0	6
Recorder's Ct.—Psychiatric	26	0	0	26
Recorder's Ct.—Traffic	279	6	0	285
Library	432	72	1	505
Total positions	21,637	2,665	1,011	25,313
Percentage of total	85.5	10.5	4.0	100.0

a. Excludes $70 million in general revenue sharing, antirecession funds, and block grant funds used for administration and services; these funds appear in the general fund columns.

local fiscal conditions. Although the CETA programs are ostensibly tied to a federal interest in employment training, the city has been able to accomplish very little training with those funds.[2] Instead, the PSE portion of CETA has been used as another source of general support for positions scattered throughout most city agencies, especially major city departments such as police, fire, and recreation.

The city clearly has substituted federal dollars for local dollars, but it must be remembered that locally available dollars have been in decline for some time, that total city employment has also been in decline, and that local tax rates have been increasing. Substitution of federal for local dollars therefore hardly reduces local taxes or prevents further tax increases. The city's desperate financial condition has forced it to grab whatever sources of support it could find to enhance general fund programs.

Use of even a "constrained" program such as PSE for general fund position support subjects these positions to a form of double jeopardy. First, if federal dollars are reduced or further restrictions on their use are added, basic city services operated by persons in PSE positions would be directly affected. Second, if another fiscal crisis forces another round of layoffs, local union rules requiring that seniority be considered in deciding whom to lay off would force the city to lay off many PSE workers with little seniority. These rules and other complications mean that the city may have federal funds it cannot spend, as in fact happened in fiscal 1978 when it was unable to spend $10 million in PSE funds. Federal funds were available, but local conditions no less than federal restrictions made their use difficult.

To a considerable extent, of course, the city's vulnerability to either federal or local revenue shortages is a function of the high wages paid to city employees. With more than 70 percent of general fund obligations allocated to salaries and fringe benefits, a less generous compensation system clearly could ease the pressure on city revenues and reduce the dimensions of the repeated crises. The city and union officials who have opted for a different course have, in effect, traded higher salaries for a smaller work force—and one that fluctuates continuously with the vagaries of uncertain funding. Figures on the number of persons actually employed by the city (as opposed to positions budgeted) show that the number

2. "Very little money received through PSE sources has been set aside for training," according to the city's "Response to the House Budget Committee's Task Force on Economic Policy Questionnaire," November 1977 (mimeo), p. 8.

of employees in most city agencies has been quite unstable since the mid-1970s. Employment in large departments such as police or fire has followed a roller coaster pattern: up when money permits, down when another crisis occurs. More than 25,000 workers were employed by the city in 1975, before the worst period of crisis began to be felt. One year later, monthly employment at times was less than 22,000. The police department, which had 6,341 employees in July 1975, was down to 4,837 in July 1976, and has since climbed as high as 6,502 before slipping back to 5,626 more recently.

Effects of the Economic Stimulus Package

The preceding discussion makes clear that the federal government's economic stimulus package has had a major, and continuing, impact on Detroit—although perhaps not exactly the intended impact. The $26 million CETA grant in fiscal 1975 came at a time when the city had entered the worst period of the 1974-75 recession, and with the addition of a public service employment component in 1976, provided assistance that helped keep the city alive during that trying period. By the spring of 1976 unemployment in Detroit began to decline, dropping to "only" 12.4 percent in August 1976 and dropping further to an annual average of 9.9 percent in 1977. The timing of these improvements is important because it establishes that the new program of antirecession fiscal assistance (ARFA), or countercyclical aid, came into place after the city's economy already had begun to improve. ARFA contributed $17.5 million to Detroit in 1977 and another $23.2 million in 1978, when unemployment was lower than it has been at any time since 1975. In 1977 and 1978, when ARFA and manpower program grants together were pouring close to $90 million and $100 million into the city treasury, the city had already passed beyond its worst recessionary period.

If these new elements of the economic stimulus package were too late to have much impact on Detroit's economic recovery, they nevertheless had a major impact on city government employment. Hundreds of laid-off workers were put back on the payroll and federal resources helped ease the path toward new union contract settlements in 1977. None of this should be taken to mean that the city was able to expand employment. The number of full-time personnel dropped by more than two thousand between July 1975 and July 1976. Millions of federal manpower and countercyclical dollars, in short, were required to do no more than maintain employment levels. This effect can hardly be regarded as a "stimulus," but its significance to Detroit city government would be difficult to exaggerate.

Although Detroit has used PSE funds as a supplement to the general fund, it has not always been easy to do so, and the 1978 amendments to federal rules governing the use of PSE funds brought about even greater difficulties. Union contracts require that PSE employees be treated in the same way as other city workers, with the same pay scales, rights of seniority, and other benefits. Before the rule changes, several hundred police officers earning salaries of between $19,000 and $24,000 were placed on PSE accounts, receiving $12,000 from title VI and the balance from the city's general fund. These salaries are higher than new federal rules permit. To complicate matters further, many of these employees have now served longer than the eighteen months allowed under the new rules, accumulating seniority that will probably protect them against layoff despite federal regulations requiring PSE layoffs when other employees are laid off. The city has obtained waivers for some of these provisions, but it has simply ignored others, falling out of compliance with federal rules. If and when the federal government chooses to enforce PSE rules strictly, the city may face both a loss of basic service personnel and an order to repay funds already spent. Given the current state of near-depression in Detroit, and another potential annual deficit of between $100 and $150 million, either penalty would be disastrous.

The third component of the economic stimulus package, the local public works program, has had important symbolic as well as economic effects in the city. Again, however, funds became available to Detroit after the worst had passed. Two billion dollars was authorized for the first round of LPW grants in 1976, during the closing days of the Ford administration; an additional $6 billion was authorized for a second round of grants during the Carter administration's first year. Detroit, as we have seen, received allocations for five projects totaling $22.4 million from round 1 and $23.8 million for twelve projects from round 2, for a total of $46.2 million. In addition, Wayne State University and the Detroit public schools received grants for use within the city limits of Detroit. Because funds in both rounds were made available in 1977, these funds could not have had an impact on the high unemployment levels of 1975-76, which were already in decline when LPW funds began to flow. Nor has the city been able to spend available LPW funds very rapidly. About $30.6 million of available LPW funds was carried into fiscal 1979.

In view of the deep-seated and long-term nature of Detroit's fiscal crisis, it is difficult to be too critical of the timing of LPW funds. The city continues to suffer from high unemployment and, if LPW money did little to alleviate the 1975-76 problem, it nevertheless was available in 1979-80, when unemployment once again began to pass from "serious" to "critical." The city's inability to spend the funds more rapidly may be a more serious problem, but it is primarily a local problem. Like other American cities, Detroit traditionally has not developed plans for capital projects until funds became available, due in large measure to the high cost of planning fees—typically between 5 and 10 percent of project costs. Although LPW rules require that construction begin within ninety days of a project award in order to retain the award, it is not clear that this rule effectively resolved the problem of planning delays. Projects in Detroit for which foundations had been poured were entitled to retain their awards, whether or not complete plans were available. Absence of completed plans caused problems in some cases during later phases of construction, further slowing the rate at which funds could be spent.

It is important to note that capital construction projects often do not have the significant effects on local employment levels that might be expected from the expenditure of such large sums of money. Detroit has followed a policy of awarding project design contracts to city-based architectural firms, but many employees of those firms are not city residents. Competitive bidding requirements for actual construction work, moreover, have allocated many contracts to noncity firms that were low bidders. Barton-Mallow, an international firm hired to manage several construction projects, opened a Detroit office only when it entered into negotiations for city work. Although outside firms typically employ local construction labor, the effect of such hiring practices on city unemployment has hardly been dramatic. The average project lasts two years and city officials estimate that 40 percent of the money goes for materials and 60 percent to labor. At the outside, therefore, the $46.2 million in LPW funds spread over two years could have generated only 700 jobs per year, assuming an average wage of $20,000 per worker—hardly enough to make a serious dent in the city's unemployment problem.

Apart from the employment effects of LPW grants or the problems associated with such grants, however, their availability has had a major symbolic significance to the city. The city's "renaissance" strategy is centered on renewal of a decayed downtown area. One first-round LPW award enabled the city to put $5 million into construction costs of the new Joe Louis Arena on the Detroit River at a time when total project funding was uncertain and when the Detroit Red Wings hockey team had announced plans to abandon the city for a new suburban arena. While the $5 million grant was less than 10 percent of total costs for the arena, it kept the project alive and helped to persuade the Red Wings to remain downtown. Since it opened in December 1979, the Louis Arena has attracted track meets, basketball tournaments, collegiate hockey tournaments, and the 1980 Republican National Convention. Similarly, a second-round grant enabled the city to obtain $5 million toward the $16 million cost of renovating Tiger Stadium, again helping persuade the city's major league baseball club to stay in the city. Other awards have gone for major reconstruction of downtown streets such as Washington Boulevard or Woodward Avenue (site of the annual Thanksgiving Day Parade), renovation of retail shopping malls, and construction of community centers. Together, these grants have given the city a sense of vitality in the downtown area that is an essential ingredient of the "renaissance" strategy.

4. Program Benefits

Grants that subsidize wealthy entrepreneurs such as the owners of
the Detroit Tigers and Red Wings raise the question of whether, in
a city with so many poor people, federal program dollars are being
delivered to those most in need of them.

The question is extraordinarily difficult to answer for several
reasons. First, programs such as general revenue sharing or antirecession fiscal assistance provide general support dollars for
normal city operations. To the extent that general city operations
benefit one income class more than another, these federal dollars
will produce similar benefit distributions. Such analyses, however, are rarely attempted and extraordinarily difficult to perform.
Moreover, determining the beneficiaries of major capital projects
can only be a matter of judgment. Detroit is refurbishing its water
system with federal support, for example, but any judgment that
one group of citizens will benefit more or less than another from
this common service is bound to be arbitrary. Finally, data necessary to provide accurate analyses are often badly outdated. The
most recent available Census Bureau data on family income as of
this writing are 1969. Using such information in estimates of the
impact of 1978 federal dollars is bound to be hazardous, particularly since we know that a population shift of some 500,000 people
took place in Detroit during that time, with unknown consequences for income distributions.

Nevertheless, the question is of sufficient interest and importance to attempt an answer, although it may be no more than a
partly informed guess. According to 1969 census figures, median
family income in Detroit was $10,038. Using this base figure, we
can define income categories and determine distributions as
shown in table 8. Because these data are available by census tract

Table 8. *Detroit Income Distribution*

Category	Definition	Percentage of city population
I	Low: 50% or less of city median income	20.06
II	Moderate: 51-80% of city median income	16.06
III	Middle: 81-120% of city median income	26.70
IV	High: 121% or more of city median income	37.18

Source: Census data.

as well, we can identify the census tracts into which program dollars were allocated and, by applying tract distributions of income classes against dollars allocated, develop an estimate of income classes benefited by various programs and for total federal dollars. Or, in the case of city employees paid with federal funds, we can identify the number of positions and salaries to develop similar estimates.

The results of these exercises are displayed in table 9, which generally suggests that most federal program dollars benefit the lowest income classes. Low-income families made up slightly more than 20 percent of the city's population in 1969, but they benefited from nearly 40 percent of federal program dollars. The lowest two income classes combined represented just over a third of the population, but they benefited from nearly two-thirds (65.2 percent) of program dollars. It should again be emphasized that some of these estimates are no more than informed guesses. Urban Mass Transportation Administration (UMTA) funds, for example, come to the city's Department of Transportation through SEMTA, and the city uses these funds to support its bus system. We know that bus users come disproportionately from low-income categories, thus we allocate larger proportions to those categories. In the case of Environmental Protection Agency (EPA) funds, we know that they are devoted largely to improving the citywide water system and, lacking a better alternative, we simply apply the citywide income distributions to those funds. On the other hand, income-tested programs such as the Elementary and Secondary Education Act (ESEA), child nutrition, or public housing can be more accurately estimated, and we can identify census tracts in

Table 9. *Percentage Distribution of Federal Program Benefits by Income Group, Fiscal 1978*

Program	Expenditures (millions of dollars)	Income category[a] I	II	III	IV	Kind of benefit
CETA title I[b]	17.3	53.8	38.5	7.7	—	Jobs
CETA title III[b]	8.1	53.8	38.5	7.7	—	Jobs
CETA STIP[b]	3.1	53.8	38.5	7.7	—	Jobs
CDBG	6.6	28.7	17.9	22.9	30.5	Services, adm.
Housing rent subsidy	8.9	100.0	—	—	—	Housing
Housing operating subsidy	5.3	100.0	—	—	—	Housing
LEAA	3.3	20.1	16.1	26.7	37.1	Services
PSE title II[c]	9.2	22.3	38.9	5.5	33.3	Jobs
PSE title VI[c]	39.0	9.0	15.7	2.2	73.1	Jobs
Urban Mass Transportation Administration[d]	16.8	47.0	28.0	15.0	10.0	Services
CDBG capital[e]	22.1	28.7	17.9	22.9	30.5	Environment
Environmental Protection Agency	27.2	20.1	16.1	26.7	37.1	Environment
LPW[e]	9.8	31.9	25.8	17.7	24.6	Environment
Elementary and Secondary Education Act	26.3	58.8	39.2	2.0	—	Services
Emergency School Assistance Act	8.5	60.0	40.0	—	—	Services
Child nutrition	16.1	58.8	39.2	2.0	—	Services
Overall average (percentage)		39.8	25.4	10.3	24.5	

Source: Data derived from the U.S. Bureau of the Census.

a. See table 8 for definitions of categories.

b. Based on target objectives.

c. City employees on PSE average above $15,000 per year. Rate for police and firefighters for FY 1978 was $14,727 to $19,271.

d. Based on the belief that low-income people benefit more from this program.

e. Based on project location by census tract.

which a number of projects are located. None of these techniques is adequate, perhaps, but all of them reinforce our conclusion that federal aid is concentrated on people with low to moderate income.

The main exceptions to this conclusion are the funds distributed through the various CETA titles. Titles I and II and the skills training and improvement program (STIP) are primarily allocated to low-income groups, largely because their principal use has been to fund part-time or temporary school or community organization workers such as school crossing guards or classroom helpers. The public service employment titles II-D and VI, however, are allocated primarily to upper-income categories. As we have shown, the city has used these funds largely to maintain employees of city agencies, whose salary scales are quite high relative to those of other city residents. Were it not for these rather high salaries, and the difficulty of estimating benefits derived by low-income citizens from the activities of city employees, the distribution of benefits would be even more skewed toward the lower income groups.

As noted earlier, some of these numbers are very old and very inaccurate. Between 1969 and 1976, median family income increased from $10,038 to $13,500, more than 300,000 (mostly white) citizens left Detroit, and more than 200,000 others (mostly black) were added to the city's population. On the reasonable, if undocumented, assumption that outmigrants have generally had higher incomes than inmigrants, we can conclude that more current data would show an even higher proportion of federal dollars allocated to the lowest income classes. This is not to say that federal funds have been "sufficient" in any sense, or even to say that the dollars have been distributed "fairly," relative to other income groups or other governmental units. These data only plausibly suggest that, in a city with a substantial number of low-income families, federal dollars are largely allocated either to those families or to areas of the city in which those families live.

5. Political Effects

There can be no doubt that the massive amounts of federal aid funneled into the city of Detroit during the past decade have enabled the city to survive as a functioning governmental unit. One could argue, of course, that survival is not necessarily a worthy result: Perhaps a massive restructuring to bring about a closer fit between services and resources would have better served the public interest. Whatever the presumptive merits of large-scale structural change, that course of action has not been pursued. Instead, the city has reduced its work force, significantly reduced its services, and sought to shift financial responsibility for selected services to the state, all the while pursuing as much state and federal assistance as possible. Federal aid has become the largest single source of local revenue by far, a political fact of major significance.

The political consequences of federal aid are particularly noticeable in the city's "renaissance" strategy, which is in turn closely associated with the incumbent mayor, Coleman A. Young. Although the $356 million Renaissance Center initiated by Henry Ford II was already under way on the Detroit riverfront when Young assumed office in 1975, the new mayor quickly made it the linchpin of his administration. This was less a matter of insight than of necessity. In an advanced state of physical and economic decline, Detroit badly needed whatever stimulus it could find. Renaissance Center was not only tangible evidence of downtown's attractiveness for investors—it remains the largest privately financed development project in the United States—but it provided a needed psychological lift for the city. Mayor Young seized this opportunity by making "Detroit Renaissance" the theme of his new administration, taking every available opportunity to seek new investments for downtown.

At the outset, neither the mayor nor his closest advisors had a clearly developed sense of strategic priorities. It was obvious to everyone that downtown was dying, that the city needed jobs, and that new private investment was crucial to long-term recovery. Turning things around was initially a matter of taking whatever was available, either in investment or outside financial help. Thus the "Moving Detroit Forward" plan developed for the April 1975 White House meeting was little more than a slick wish list, compiled from agency ideas of "good things to do" and a few big ideas from the mayor's staff. That document was nevertheless extremely important politically. For one thing, it provided an opportunity for the mayor to exercise his considerable persuasive skills to put together a powerful coalition of economic and governmental leaders, focused on the problem of city revitalization. For another, the process of generating this wish list helped to clarify city purposes and crystallize a strategy that was feasible as well as desirable. It gradually became clear that the city would vigorously pursue downtown development, placing heavier emphasis on massive public investment in a new subway system to generate both jobs and further private investment in the long run. At the same time the city would seek to stem the tide of population loss by identifying neighborhoods in which new public investments could either enhance the quality of viable areas or prevent further decay in transitional neighborhoods. Implementation of this two-pronged strategy, relying extensively on federal aid, has significantly enhanced the political power of the mayor.

If the key to downtown revitalization is the proposed Detroit subway, the key to actual construction of a subway is the support provided by an extraordinary coalition of economic and governmental leaders in which Mayor Young is the central figure. A Detroit subway, of course, would be unthinkable without a commitment of massive federal support: originally a $600 million commitment from President Ford, later increased to $900 million by President Carter. Federal assistance, however, depends on local (that is, metropolitan) agreement on a plan for the subway system, and funding support from the state legislature. Given conflicts between the economic interests of the city and those of its suburbs, magnified by severe racial tensions between a largely black city and overwhelmingly white suburbs, obstacles to the plan must have seemed insurmountable. Yet, after years of wrangling, the city and suburban representatives on the board of

SEMTA agreed on a plan in April 1980, and two months later the legislature appropriated funds for the necessary preliminary engineering studies. Not a shovel has been turned to date, but, five years after the initial federal commitment, a Detroit subway seems on its way.

If so, the mayor and his elite coalition are largely responsible. Corporate leaders, particularly those now housed in the Renaissance Center, whose employees are certain to be major users of a line running down Woodward Avenue from the suburbs, provided support, as did the unions which presumably benefit from a massive and lengthy construction project. The Detroit *Free Press* repeatedly provided strong editorial endorsement. Governor Milliken and his staff lobbied hard in the legislature, working closely with the mayor and his staff to ultimately win support even from outstate legislators, many of whom had retained close relationships with Young from his years in the state senate. The deals struck to gain support in Lansing may never be fully known, but the suburban opponents to the subway proposal clearly were no match for this powerful coalition orchestrated by Young.

Strong corporate support for a black mayor who spent his early years as a union organizer may seem incongruous, but it is hardly accidental. The mayor's interest in economic revitalization has led him to seek corporate assistance and to be extremely solicitous of business interests. During his first term he persuaded most of the city's prominent corporate leaders to participate in an advisory Economic Growth Council. In February 1978 this group was formalized as the Detroit Economic Growth Corporation, which now operates on a million-dollar budget partly supplied by city funds. The mayor also strongly supported a Downtown Development District, which permits taxes generated through downtown investments to be retained exclusively for further downtown development.

Even before large amounts of federal aid were available, the mayor began liberal use of Michigan Public Law 198 (1974) that permits local governments to provide tax abatements for industry. As of summer 1980, nearly two hundred abatement requests had been approved by the city, in some cases against significant council opposition. When federal money for downtown renewal began to be available, primarily in the form of urban development action grants and local public works grants, the mayor made major commitments to downtown developments organized by many coalition members: J.L. Hudson for Cadillac Square, A. L. Taubman and

Max Fisher for a riverfront apartment complex, General Motors for neighborhood renewal, the Tigers and Red Wings for stadium renewal or construction, and so on.

Mayor Young, in short, has sought out corporate advice, cultivated corporate support through federal financial assistance, and used corporate influence when possible to build momentum for continued downtown development. In the process he has built a firm alliance with the city's economic elite.

These kinds of projects have been much ballyhooed as evidence of the city's rejuvenation but, however rich and influential corporations may be, they do not vote. People vote, and they are especially likely to vote if they are organized. As a former community activist as well as union organizer, Young has seen to it that substantial sums of federal assistance have been poured into neighborhoods, particularly from the community development block grant program. From May 1975 to June 1980, according to the Planning Department, about 78 percent of all community development funds were allocated to neighborhood and housing development projects, a sharp contrast with grants made under the urban development action grant (UDAG) programs, in which 57 percent of funds awarded went to projects located downtown. The Community Services Agency and HEW health grants have also been largely allocated to Detroit neighborhoods, providing substantial resources for the mayor to use in cultivating grassroots support.

The care with which neighborhood support has been cultivated is especially evident in city allocations of CDBG funds. HUD requires a plan before CDBG funds are released but the plan is a local, not a federal product. In Detroit, where Mayor Young is the dominant decision maker in all capital projects, some fifteen neighborhood strategy areas have been targeted for intensive CDBG investments, but substantial sums have been funneled into neighborhood retail centers, housing, and service improvements all over the city. Even more interesting is the use of CDBG funds to provide staff assistance for citizens district councils as well as general support for neighborhood groups. The city has provided funds to about forty-three neighborhood organizations, including some—such as the Michigan Avenue Citizens Organization ($150,000)—that have been highly critical of the mayor in past years. CDBG budget allocations from the neighborhood opportunity fund to these organizations in fiscal 1979 ranged from $15,000 to $300,000, but also include $5.5 million in "unallocated" funds, providing a substantial pot from which to generate continuing political support or co-opt opponents. With a large and expanding network of neighborhood organizations that have benefited from their interactions with the mayor, a fund of federal money available to nourish this network, and a political style that is enormously popular among a largely black electorate, the mayor has created a base of electoral support that seems very secure indeed.

Whether or not one agrees with the mayor's priorities or his uses of federal funds, it is important to grasp the quality of the political change he has engineered. Before Young, the city's economic elite was highly concentrated but given to "lone ranger" activities in Detroit. Walker Cisler of Detroit Edison tried and failed on his own to develop a "new-town-in-town" around Edison Plaza; Henry Ford II has largely succeeded in developing a new town outside Detroit in Dearborn; J.L. Hudson has ringed the city with independently planned shopping centers. Young's achievement has been to transform a "do-your-own-thing" elite into a coalition that is focused on the city, able to coordinate its influence, and organized to work cooperatively. Before Young, the city's nonpartisan electoral system enabled the newspapers and the UAW to exert considerable electoral power, but undermined the development of a stable electoral base for a chief executive. Young's achievement has been to broaden his own electoral base and stabilize it. Before Young, the city's largely independent civil service often hindered coordinated city action. Young's achievement has been to use new resources to focus and organize city government programs. Young is clearly a man of consummate political skill but, skill aside, none of these achievements would have been possible without the resources provided by federal money.

Coleman A. Young, in short, has organized Detroit. There is now someone in charge who can make things happen and who can assume responsibility. The executive-centered coalition of corporate leaders, labor, voters, and the city bureaucracy itself is a more centralized and coherent system of power than the city had a decade ago, and the city thus has a higher capacity to act purposively than it had a decade ago. This coalition also has a relatively clear sense of city purposes—developed opportunistically, to be sure, but nevertheless widely understood and shared. Because rebuilding the economic infrastructure of the city through massive public and private investment stands at the center of city aspirations, perhaps the most important quality of this new system of power is its apparent stability. Young, who has had attractive opportunities to move "up" to Washington, appears to have decided to remain committed to Detroit. So long as he remains, and maintains his power base, potential investors will have a basis for predicting and responding to city actions. If political predictability can affect investment decisions, this is no small advantage.

The major weakness of this power system, of course, is its highly personalized structure. Young himself holds most of his coalitions together, through a combination of intelligence, flamboyance, aggressiveness, and money; this combination would be impossible to duplicate. Although Young's current operational style is reminiscent of the machine operated for decades by Chicago Mayor Richard Daley, it lacks one crucial ingredient Daley could rely on: a growing number of city jobs to hand out. Nor has the Young machine identified and publicized likely successors to the mayor, if and when he steps down. Whether Young's network of community-based organizations could be maintained by a successor, or whether the elite coalitions could or would support a successor, are thus open questions.

A personalized political system kept together in good measure by skillful use of externally generated funds seems likely to be fragile if external funds diminish. Detroit's underlying fiscal distress will not soon go away—indeed, the decline of the American automobile industry is certain to deepen that distress. Any significant reduction in federal funds, therefore, would force the city to immediately consider further service and personnel reductions, further shifts of service responsibilities to other governmental jurisdictions, further increases in an already burdensome system of local taxes, or some combination of all of these measures. Mayor Young is likely to seek and gain reelection, but even his skills would be severely tested in coping simultaneously with huge deficits and major losses in federal revenues. Detroit will survive its deficits with or without federal assistance, but the price of survival may well be significant political and governmental change.

6. Conclusions

The city of Detroit's official seal, adopted in 1827, commemorates an 1805 fire with dual mottos: "It shall rise again from the ashes" and "We hope for better things." Ashes of decay, social disorganization, or abandonment are sprinkled liberally around this old city, but it is not yet clear that anything accomplished during the past decade of energetic fiscal politics will cause the city to rise again from those ashes. Renaissance Center is a gleaming new centerpiece for downtown, to be sure, but people continue to abandon the city, and the city's principal industry seems to be moving toward significant retrenchment. Despite two decades of major national policy initiatives and national court actions, furthermore, the Detroit area is more segregated by race and class divisions than ever before. City officials have struggled furiously to deal with these problems but they remain and, in a recessionary period, are becoming worse. What is left, therefore, is what is on the other side of the city seal: hope.

Although largely an intangible resource, the hope that currently permeates Detroit's leadership structure has a base of real accomplishment. Having organized for joint action, the city's institutional leaders have a growing confidence that they can work together because they already have done so, in Lansing and Washington as well as in the city itself. And, while little progress has been made on major problems such as unemployment or racial hostilities, a string of successful projects, particularly in the downtown area, has created a momentum that can be extended. If major investors can be persuaded, finally, to join the Cadillac Center and Woodward Mall projects downtown, if riverfront housing plans can also attract investors, and if the subway project moves forward with its billion-dollar federal contribution, the momentum of small successes during the past half-decade can easily develop into a flood of new money and new jobs. These are big "ifs," but the plans are in place and the power structure is committed to action.

Massive amounts of federal aid have ensured the city's survival during a period when even hope seemed unreasonable. The more important effect of federal assistance, however, has been to provide resources, available nowhere else, that a competent city leadership has been able to use to generate a strategy for city revitalization. In this sense, federal money, because it has been provided for so wide a range of programs and with so few conditions attached, has provided strong support for the principle of local responsibility and local accountability for problem solving. Whether or not Detroit succeeds in transforming its economic base, the contribution made by federal assistance to strengthening Detroit's capacity for local governance must be regarded as a major political effect. If Detroit succeeds, the federal dollars poured into the city in recent years will be seen as a very good investment indeed.

7. Epilog

Detroit's economic and fiscal decline continued unabated during 1979 and 1980. The continuing slump in automobile sales fed high levels of unemployment while unprecedented interest rates brought other sectors of the regional economy—particularly the housing industry—to a virtual halt. Detroiters who could flee to the more active job markets of the Southwest did so; many of those who remained put increasing pressure on available welfare and social support services. Under these conditions the city was unable to generate enough revenue to balance its precarious budget, which continued to run a deficit that approached, then exceeded, $100 million. By 1981 it had become clear that, unless radical action were taken, a fiscal 1981 deficit of $120 million would be followed by an even larger deficit of $150 million in fiscal 1982. Suddenly the fiscal gap between resources and expenditure requirements had not only breached the $200 million level, but seemed on its way toward $300 million.

Efforts to cope with the city's deepening crisis focused initially on Lansing, but the state budget was itself under severe pressure, for many of the same reasons that had caused the city's fiscal decline. In the spring of 1981, with state programs and state employment being reduced, significant increases in assistance to Detroit seemed out of the question. Instead, Mayor Young and Governor Milliken worked out a series of proposals the governor was later to call a "self-help, self-discipline" plan for Detroit. The plan drew in part on the experience of New York City (Felix Rohatyn, the investment banker who was a chief architect in that city's recovery, was called in to consult with Detroit officials) and in part on labor-management innovations recently implemented in settling the financial difficulties of the Chrysler Corporation. The plan authorized the city to hold a special election on June 23, 1981 to increase the city income tax from 2 to 3 percent for residents and from 0.5 to 1.5 percent for nonresidents who work in the city.

If voters approved the tax increase, the plan's other provisions would go into effect. These provisions did the following:

1. Authorized the city to issue up to $125 million in long-term bonds to help eliminate the estimated $120 million fiscal 1981 deficit, and required the city to show that buyers for such bonds were available.
2. Required the city to obtain wage concessions from unionized city employees in order to balance the budget.
3. Required the city to submit a balanced budget for fiscal 1982 to the State Administrative Board by August 15, 1981.
4. Required the city to submit a balanced budget for fiscal 1983 to the State Administrative Board by June 15, 1982.

From the city's point of view, this package seemed quite drastic. Not only were city voters to be asked to increase their own burden substantially during a period of near depression, but even if they agreed, the State Administrative Board, composed of the governor, treasurer, and other senior state officers, was to become a partner in managing the fiscal affairs of the city. The burden this plan imposed on the mayor seemed even more serious, perhaps even impossible. If he could persuade hard-pressed city residents to raise their taxes, he would gain no more than the opportunity to persuade bankers to support a large bond issue and a mandate to somehow persuade militant city unions to accept unspecified wage concessions—all before August 15. A more difficult set of tasks for a big-city mayor would be hard to imagine.

Nonetheless Mayor Young vigorously supported the legislation, against the equally vigorous opposition of the city's unions, suburban legislators whose constituents would pay a higher city tax, and upstate legislators whose belief in the mismanagement of city affairs remained unshaken. The tax increase authorization passed the Michigan House by a vote of fifty-six to fifty on June 4. Governor Milliken spent much of the next day calling Republican senators to urge their support in the Senate and, after six hours of debate and two unfavorable Senate votes on the bill, the Senate tried again, only to produce a tied vote, nineteen to nineteen. In a moment of high political drama, Lieut. Gov. James Brickley then cast the decisive vote, as presiding officer of the Senate, in favor of the legislation. By a single vote Detroit had gained the right to ask its citizens to raise taxes.

The campaign that followed was a model of mayoral skill in coalition management. Although city unions and a suburban coalition campaigned hard against the tax increase, they were overwhelmed by a massive media blitz funded by more than $400,000 contributed by members of Mayor Young's business and industrial coalition. As the campaign wore on, it gradually became a referendum on Mayor Young himself, as defender of the city's right to maintain control over its own affairs—a position the mayor exploited with great skill among the predominantly black constituency. Showing exquisite political timing, the mayor announced a new three-year contract with the Detroit Police Officers Association on Monday, June 22, the day before the special election. The agreement froze police salaries for two years, but it also provided a guarantee against police layoffs. In return, the union endorsed the tax proposal. Since the DPOA long had been the most militant of the city unions, the photo of a smiling mayor and union president that graced the front page of the Detroit *Free Press* on election day, June 23, was a signal to voters that even the mayor's most vigorous opponents understood the need to "Vote *For* Detroit." The tax increase passed easily.

With two-thirds of the electorate behind him, the mayor held a strong hand. One by one the city's unions agreed to new contracts that typically imposed a two-year freeze on wages. When the largest union—the American Federation of State, County, and Municipal Employees (AFSCME)—refused to accept this scheme in July, the city's budget director promptly announced that 428 AFSCME members would be laid off on August 1 and that as many as a thousand nonuniformed employees would probably lose their jobs unless wages could be frozen. AFSCME members soon reconsidered, and union agreements to freeze wages were all in place by August 15. So too were agreements with local banks and public employee pension funds, who agreed to provide markets for the bonds required to eliminate the $120 million deficit. On August 15, therefore, the city could assure the state that the current budget was in balance and that a projected deficit would be eliminated by a combination of new taxes and wage stabilization agreements. Difficult as they had appeared less than two months earlier, the tasks of raising local taxes, cutting city expenditures, and floating bonds to cover a large deficit had all been achieved.

Although Mayor Young and his coalition supporters argued strongly that these measures would restore long-term fiscal solvency to Detroit, recent reductions in federal assistance programs seem certain to undermine that hope. As of September 1981, state officials were estimating that about $86 million in federal revenue would be lost to the state in programs such as AFDC, food stamps, medicaid, and social services grants, $56 million would be lost in CETA and Community Service Administration grants, and $12 million in health services, alcohol abuse, and maternal care grants. All of these programs have concentrated their expenditures very noticeably in cities like Detroit. It is entirely conceivable, therefore, that the city may face another $100 million deficit in a few months, this time composed of a shortfall in federal rather than local dollars. Whether this hard-pressed and struggling city will find another avenue toward fiscal solvency remains an open question. One conclusion, however, seems apparent from the record of the past decade: It will try.